Mission is birthed from the heart of God, who sends His son to die on the cross for reconciling humanity that brings into existence the church which is empowered and compelled by love poured in believers' hearts by the Holy Spirit. Message from Heart of God to Heart of Believer gives meaning, purpose and confidence to engage with the world. This is a great, concise book on Missions with academic integrity, practical wisdom and action-oriented discussion questions. This book can move young people into missions. This can be used in small groups, youth groups, institutions, and academic institutions.

J. N. Manokaran
South Asia Regional Director
Community Bible Study International

Dr Saji K Lukos and Brother Salim Pani deserves much appreciation for their endeavors to provide a concise study material on Christian missions for the lay-Christians leaders and beginners at the Bible Colleges for ministerial training. He discussed the missional components in ten distinctive fragments from scriptural and social points of view so as to cover up from the heart of God to the heart of the world with an aim to instill in them zeal to carry on God's Mission in the pluralistic context of India. This book could be used as one of the textbooks for the Mission India Bible Colleges.

Dr Hruda Ranjan Lohora
Dean of Academics (Mission India Theological Seminary)

"Building God's Kingdom: Introduction to Christian Missions" is the outcome of wide reading, careful thinking and relevant to the need of the 21st century in India. Dr Saji Lukos, an experienced mission leader, founder and a profound writer teamed up with the dynamic young leader Mr Salim Pani brought this book. This book is a combination of real originality with intellectual integrity. This book will be a great help to the cross cultural missionaries, mission leaders to reach the unreached in this 21st century.

Dr J. Ganesapandy
Professor of Missiology at Mission India
Theological Seminary, Nagpur
Cross-cultural missionary among the korkus in
Amravati district of Maharashtra, India and Mission Educator

"Mission arises from the heart of God himself," says C. J. H Wright. The avowal vividly describes the prominence of mission and the need for understanding it by knowing the heart of God. I am happy to learn my friend and leader Dr Saji K. Lukos and team wrote a basic textbook on Christian Missions aiming at the emerging lay leaders, teachers, and Bible students. I strongly believe that the book titled, "Building God's Kingdom: Introduction to Christian Mission," will be an unavoidable addition to the field of mission studies and will benefit to many. To study more about missions are very much inevitable in the present Christian mission scenario. I wish and pray that more collection shall come through his wisdom.

Rev. P. D. Joseph
Chief Functionary
Mission India, Nagpur

Christian Heritage Rediscovered

The Series, as the name suggests, is meant to focus on Christian Faith & Living vis-à-vis topics like Literature & Poetry, Indigenous Philosophizing, Ethical response towards Agriculture, Health & Healing, Science & Technology, Ecofeminist Theology, Sociological approach towards Human Rights, Law & Politics, Arts, History of Ideas, Ancient Civilizations, Cultural Contiguity, Religious Cosmologies & Mysticism, Footsteps of famous Theologians, World Peace & Harmony, Global Capitalism, Network Marketing, Cybertheology, Population & Demographics, Epigraphic Studies, Contextualized Education, and many others. We welcome a Mss. on any topic/s mentioned, whether they are original works, scholarly monographs, collections of conference papers, revised dissertations, or translations of historical documents. Through the Series we, the Publishers, are striving to put forward published works that may help Institutions, Academic Bodies, Researchers, Scholars and the World at large in furthering their respective knowledge and understanding on the concerned subject. We welcome your comments on our efforts and further suggestions on how we can foster the upcoming thoughtful theologically grounded books.

Christian Heritage Rediscovered - 85

Building God's Kingdom

Introduction to Christian Missions

Edited by
Saji K. Lukos
Salim Tapan Pani

CWI
Christian World Imprints

First Published in 2019 by

Christian World Imprints
Christian Publishing & Books from India
C-3, Shop No. 14, Ground Floor
Wazirpur Industrial Area, **Delhi-110052**
cwidelhi2017@gmail.com
www.ChristianWorldImprints.com
Phone: +91 11 41526079

ISBN: 978-93-5148-385-4 (HB)
ISBN: 978-93-5148-386-1 (PB)

Printed in India.

Contents

Preface

Mission proceeds from the very heart of God. His love for the lost and efforts for reconciliation with the fallen humankind is absolutely remarkable. Since the fall of Adam and Eve, He is continuously making intentional efforts by sending His agents of peace. The human history has witnessed God's enabling power in and through the lives of many saints who dedicated themselves for the accomplishment of His Mission to reach each human hearts. God convinced me of His eternal love and graciously instilled His vision to reach the unreached places in India, South Asia and beyond by developing Christ-like leaders. It is beyond my imagination to consider myself worthy for His divine mission. But, God's enabling grace sustained me and Mission India/RIMI came into existence as an obedience to our Master's call to serve the humankind.

Past 25 years is a journey of listening attentively to our Lord's voice and walking tirelessly on His footsteps. Even though, this journey was marked with constant challenges of many kinds in the mission field, but, His super natural intervention and enigmatic provision was always on time. Fast few decades have taught me to discern God's movement among the communities of India and constant engagement with the fellow mission workers, church planters and several Christian organizations provided the necessary insights to understand the core need of these communities. Since the inception, Mission India exists to study the communities, understand God's move and engage in God's mission promptly. Apart from my other publications, I had the desire to accumulate the learned insights of past missional experiences in the light of existing resources on Christian Missions and publish it in a book format. I am grateful to God for this opportunity to produce an understandable and an introductory book on Christian Missions. Mr Salim Tapan Pani joined me on this endeavor and contributed significant insights from his theological and missional experiences.

The primary objective of this book is to facilitate the missional learning of the missionaries, church planters, beginners at the seminaries and the lay Christian leaders, so that they will be more effective and updated in their efforts. Action oriented questions are mentioned in each chapters for the readers to reflect and create an environment of productive discussion. It is my sincere prayer to the Lord that, He will speak to His people through the reading of this book and lead them to accomplish the divine calling in and through their lives. May the Lord of Harvest enable you through His grace to accomplish great things for this nation.

Dr Saji K Lukos
Founder and President
Mission India, Nagpur

General Introduction

I am indebted to God for enabling missiologists, mission practitioners and lay Christian leaders to pen down significant resources on Christian missions. They have contributed at large to encourage us to seek God's heart for the humankind, discern the divine moves of God among nations and the current trends and shifts in the missional realm. It is my privilege to be part of this endeavor to develop a working material/basic introductory book on Christian missions. The first four chapters are contributed by Dr Saji K Lukos and I could pen down the rest of the chapters of the book. We believe that many will be benefited and be led to get closer to God's mission and further implement their learning for the expansion of God's kingdom.

As this book compiles the basics of Christian missions, attempts has been made to facilitate the readers to understand the key missional themes in the scripture and their implications for the Christian missions in the context of India. A set of questions mentioned at the end of each chapter will assist the readers to be able to reflect on their learning and encourage them to discuss in a group. The book begins with some of the trending definitions and terminologies existing in the Christian missions today. These key terms in missions emerged out of missional reflections of people and acts as the primary pointers to understand missions in its context. Missions emerge from the missionary heart of God. The ultimate source to seek God's heart is to go back to the scripture. So, it is absolutely necessary that, we establish the foundations of our missions and derive inspiration for continuity from the Scripture alone.

The Old Testament testifies of a God who expresses His deepest love and concern for the restoration of the fallen humankind. From the beginning of Genesis, God relentlessly approaches His people by sending individuals. The New Testament records His ultimate gift of salvation for the humankind through Jesus Christ. With the sacrifice of Jesus Christ, God reconciled the humankind to Himself. Jesus' birth, death and resurrection proves God's definite mission for the world. First few chapters of this book talks about the major themes of missions found in the scripture. God's selection of His people to bring salvation for the entire world, making them as a witnessing community during the exile, Jesus' divine mission and his great commission, the Holy Spirit enabling the first century believers and apostles for the missions …are some of the key aspects highlighted in these chapters. The church being the agent of transformation on this earth, acts as the significant source from the beginning of the early Christianity. The foundation and inspiration of church emerges from the scripture itself. It is also equally important to understand the relationship between the church and the Christian missions today. These two chapters on the topic, 'the church and Christian missions and the kingdom of God' will provide the readers with the foundational principles of these two key entities and their irreplaceable significance towards God's missions on earth. Missions without understanding and relying on the scripture will not produce any result. Moreover, scripturally authenticated missions make possible attempts to align their strategies to root themselves in the divine word of God.

Having said the significance of scriptural inspiration for Christian missions, this book also talks of the sociological and cultural aspects of Christian missions in the context of India. The current development on urbanizations and migration has caused sociological and cultural challenges. So, our missional efforts must pay attention to such changes occurring in the society. Missions are meant for the people and for the society. The later chapters of this book discusses on the subjects of the holistic missions, intercultural learning skills required for mission workers, significance of relevant contextualization and church's preparedness to minister among the migrant communities. Scripturally authenticated, sociologically driven missions have the potential to identify the issues of the society and effectively make difference for the expansion of God's kingdom on earth. I personally believe that, the readers of the book will receive some valuable insights for their engagement in Christian missions.

Salim Tapan Pani
Mission India, Nagpur

Chapter 1

Important Terms Used in Mission

It is very important for students of missions to understand the basic definitions of various terminologies in missions. Below are basic definitions without detailed descriptions.

1. Mission

Mission refers to everything the church does to advance the kingdom of God. It is not just the Great Commission (i.e., evangelism and discipleship). It includes the holistic ministry of the church.

2. Missions

Missions in the broader sense emphasizes the Great Commission of the Lord Jesus Christ (Matthew 28:18-20), proclaiming the Good News in word and deed with the goal of changing lives in order to establish replicating, Christ-centered communities, all for the glory of God.

"Missions is a specialized term. By it I mean the sending forth of authorized persons beyond the borders of the New Testament church and her immediate gospel influence to proclaim the gospel of Jesus

Christ in gospel-destitute areas, to win converts from other faiths or non-faiths to Jesus Christ, and to establish functioning, multiplying local congregations who will bear the fruit of Christianity in that community and to that country."[1]

"Mission is the intentional crossing of barriers from Church to non-church in word and deed for the sake of the proclamation of the Gospel."[2]

Missions is "an enterprise devoted to proclaiming the Good News of Jesus Christ, and to persuading men to become His disciples and dependable, reproductive members of His Church."[3]

3. *Missio Dei*

The term missio Dei (from Latin, meaning "God's mission") has meant the Inner-Trinitarian process of sending, originally found in Catholic dogmatics and particularly since St. Augustine. The World Missionary Conference held in Willingen in 1952 adopted the term for the Protestant realm in order to illustrate that world missions efforts are rooted in the Trinitarian nature of God. Georg F. Vicedom made the term popular through his book Missio Dei (1958). In the New Testament, the sending of the disciples by Jesus is understood to be an extension of the sending of Jesus by his Father (Matthew 10:40; Mark 9:37; Luke 9:48; 10:16; Acts 3:20, 26; approx. 50 times in John; comp. as far back as in the Old Testament, Isaiah 48:16) and the sending of the Holy Spirit by the Father and Jesus (John 14:26; 15:26; Luke 24:49) and for that reason uses the same words for 'to send,' 'sending,' etc. (Latin: missio) (particularly John 17:18; 20:21.[4] It emphasizes the purpose that God has assigned to the church as a means to know, love and serve Him and be happy with Him forever in heaven.

---

[1] George Peters, *A Biblical Theology of Missions* (Chicago: Moody Press, 1984), np.

[2] Stephen Neill, "How my mind has changed about mission", Video recording produced by Oversees Ministries Study Center, 1984.

[3] Donald A. McGavran, *Understanding Church Growth* (Michigan: Wm. B. Eerdmans Publishing Company, 1980), 26.

[4] Thomas Schirrmacher, "Lexikon des Christentums," in Harenberg Lexikon der Religion (Düsseldorf: Harenberg Verlag, 2002), 196 (keyword "Missio Dei").

4. Missiology

Missiology is the study of missions, mission and Missio Dei. Missiology has three central concerns:

a. The Identity or Nature of mission
b. The Goal of mission
c. The Means and Method of mission.

To fulfill those concerns, missiology includes the study of the nature of God, the created world, and the church, and the ways these all interact."[5]

5. Missionary

Missionary, "Apostle (one who is sent)" is an agent of God to share the love of God through words and deeds both locally and globally, totally obedient to the calling, and trusted in the power of the Holy Spirit for transforming lives and communities. "A missionary is a prepared disciple whom God sends into the world with His resources to make disciples for his kingdom."[6]

A missionary is "a ministering agent, selected by God and His church, to communicate the gospel message across any and all cultural boundaries for the purpose of leading people to Christ and establishing them into viable fellowships that are also capable of reproducing themselves." Ray Tallman, Introduction to World Mission.

6. 10/40 Window

This is an imaginary rectangular window proposed by missiologist Dr Luis Bush between the 10th and 40th latitudes, bordered around the Middle East and Asia. This window contains the bulk of the unreached peoples in the world and the bulk of non-Christian religions.

---

[5] A. Scott Moreau, Gary R. Corwin, Gary B. McGee, *Introducing World Missions: A Biblical, Historical, and Practical Survey* (Grand Rapids: Baker publishing group, 2004), 17.

[6] Ada Lum, *A Hitchhiker's Guide to Missions* (Downers Grove: Intervarsity Press, 1984), 21.

7. Contextualization

This refers to the presentation of the Good News in the context of the people in such a way that the people can understand and incorporate or embody the message for life transformation. It is more than just theology; it also includes developing church life and ministry that are biblically faithful and culturally relevant. It is important to be careful to avoid any kind of *syncretism* in the process of cultural adaptation.

Contextualization involves an attempt to present the Gospel in a culturally relevant way.[7] We need to be ethically sound in our evangelistic methodology (2 Corinthians 4:2). Becoming all things to all men in an incarnational approach does not necessitate an ethical breach. Jesus instructed His disciples to be as "wise as serpents, and harmless as doves" (Matthew 10:16). We are to be wise in our bridge building. We are to be harmless in our integrity as we hold forth the truth.[8]

8. Syncretism

Syncretism, as defined by the American Heritage Dictionary, is "the reconciliation or fusion of differing systems of belief."[9] This is most evident in the areas of philosophy and religion, and usually results in a new teaching or belief system. Obviously, this cannot be reconciled to biblical Christianity.

Religious syncretism often takes place when foreign beliefs are introduced to an indigenous belief system and the teachings are blended. The new, heterogeneous religion then takes a shape of its own. This has been seen most clearly in Roman Catholic missionary history. Take, for example, the Roman Catholic Church's proselytizing of animistic South America. Threatened with the fear of death, natives were baptized into the church by the tens of thousands without any preaching of the Gospel whatsoever. Former temples were razed, with Catholic shrines and chapels built on the same spot.

---

[7] Edward D Andrews, "Reasoning from the Scriptures: Sharing Christ as you help others to learn about the mighty works of God" (USA: Christian Publishing House, 2018), 36.

[8] christianitytoday.com/edstetzer/2014/october/what-is-contextualization.

[9] American Heritage Dictionary.

Natives were allowed to substitute praying to saints instead of gods of water, earth and air, and replaced their former idols with new images of the Roman Catholic Church.

Religious syncretism is simply not compatible with true Christianity. In fact, any modification to biblical law and principle for the sake of a "better" religion is heresy (Revelation 22:18-19).[10]

9. Culture

Culture is defined as a collective way of life for a specific group passed on from generation to generation through a highly adaptive array of symbols, practices, behaviors, and values that enable them to create and enjoy a world that God has provided.

Various Levels of Culture

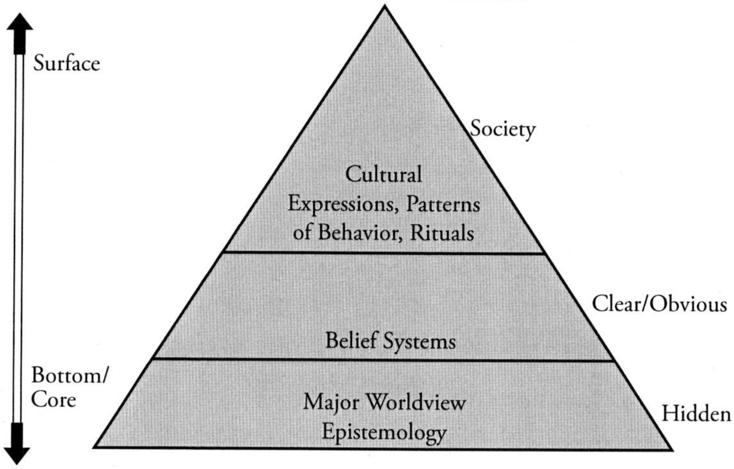

10. Incarnational Mission

This is defined as the way of living like Christ, who "was made flesh," to reach the people in a new context. Following the example of Christ, missionaries need to incarnate themselves into their new context so that they can learn the language and culture of their new context in order to present the Gospel effectively. They live out the life that Christ puts in them, bearing fruit unto God, by means of the Holy Spirit dwelling in them.

[10] gotquestions.org/syncretism-religious.

11. Indigenous Church

A church that fits well into the local culture. It is defined in four *self*-self-supporting, self-governing, self-propagating, and self-theologizing (the ability to develop its own theological understandings from the Scripture through the revelation of Jesus by the indwelling Holy Spirit).

12. Indigenous Missionary

An indigenous missionary is a missionary who is serving people with the message of the Gospel either within the local or foreign context. One example is an Odisha missionary reaching his own people in his state. He is also a cross-cultural missionary when he crosses his cultural boundaries to reach the people in Jammu Kashmir.

13. Majority World

It is a term used to describe the non-Westernized world including the developing world, Africa, Asia, the two-thirds world, the underdeveloped world, and World A. Today the church is growing exponentially in the Majority World as they send missionaries to the nations. Today, the Pew Forum study finds, "more than 1.3 billion Christians live in the Global South [61% of all Christians live in Asia, Africa, and Latin America], compared with about 860 million in the Global North (39%)."

14. People Groups

A people group is defined by ethnic or linguistic terms to be a homogenous people with the same culture, values and behavior. It is estimated that there are some 12,000 distinct languages and dialects and as many as 24,000 people groups in the world today. For example, according to Joshua Project, there are 289 people groups in Jammu and Kashmir, and 279 of these are still considered to be unreached people groups.

15. Unreached People Groups

People groups that currently have no or little access to the Gospel. They are unable to hear the Gospel in their own language and context in a way that makes sense and is understandable to them.

16. Tent making

This is defined as the practice of using paid employment to gain and maintain entry in a cross-cultural setting. Tentmakers work as professionals and engage in ministry activities in addition to doing their secular work. This was the method Paul used in Corinth by supporting himself and helping his companions by making tents while serving Christ in order to build His kingdom.

17. Transformation

It is the effort of working to change society by transforming its unjust structures into more just ones. It is the responsibility of the missionaries to be "salt and light" by developing transformational programs to enable people to develop for the glory of God through the outworking of the Spirit of Christ in them. Historically, missionaries worked to transform societies by fighting against slave trade, infanticide, upper body clothes controversy, child marriage, sati culture etc…

18. Biblical Mandate

Woven throughout God's Word is a redemptive thread, which reveals God's heart is to bring all peoples, nations and tongues to salvation through faith in Jesus Christ. The mandate or command is that every believer be involved in this process of taking the message of the Gospel to the nations (see Genesis 12:1-3; Psalm 96:3; Matthew 28:18-20; Mark 16:15; Luke 24:45-49; John 20:21; Acts 1:8).

19. Closed country

A country whose government or regime has closed it to some major form of Christian ministry from outside, such as resident foreign missionaries, visiting evangelists, freely distributed Scriptures, Christian literature, tapes or videos or films, or other Christian influences from outside of that closed country.

20. Viable Indigenous Church

Within an ethnolinguistic people or a mini-people, an indigenous community of believing Christians with adequate numbers and resources to evangelize their own people group without necessitating outside (cross-cultural) assistance.

21. World Evangelization

The term used for the goal of reaching the entire world with the Gospel of Christ, giving every people group and population on earth the opportunity to hear and comprehend the Gospel and to become disciples of Christ.

22. World A

In the 3-tier schema of the Earth, the unevangelized world, i.e., the world of all unevangelized individuals.

23. World B

In the 3-tier schema of the Earth, the evangelized non-Christian world, i.e., all non-Christians who have nevertheless become evangelized.

24. World C

In the 3-tier schema of the Earth, the Christian world, i.e., the world of all who individually are Christians.

25. Worldview

A set of presuppositions which we hold (consciously or unconsciously) about the basic make-up of our world; the central assumptions, beliefs, concepts, premises and values which are shared by a community. Because of the widespread acceptance of these assumptions within the society, these ideas are usually regarded as being nonnegotiable and beyond dispute. Worldview has been compared to glasses through which a community of people views reality. For example, if a people believes that a supernatural spiritual realm controls natural events (animism), they will draw different conclusions about an event from someone who does not believe in a supernatural realm.

Chapter 2

Missions in the Old Testament

It is essential for Christians to understand the basis for missions in the Bible so that they will be able to stand for the purpose of God with love, courage and humility. Obedience to God comes by knowing the Truth; Jesus is the Truth. The Bible begins with the Old Testament. It is a missionary book. Many Christians avoid the mission mandate in the Old Testament by only emphasizing mission in the New Testament. However, without the Old Testament, there is no New Testament. Both reveal the heart of our missionary God.

God's Missionary Role in the Old Testament[11]

From the very beginning God has been involved in the spiritual and material welfare of the world. We see this in the creation story (Genesis 1-2).

[11] Used notes from Christian Missions in Biblical Perspective, J. Herbert Kane, Baker House, Grand Rapids, MI, 1976.

1. God is the Creator and Sustainer of the Physical Universe

The Old Testament begins with the magnificent declaration of Genesis 1:1. This is sufficient grounds for Christian mission. Because God made the world, He owns it. It is His. Let us meditate on/discuss the following:

Psalm 95:4-5____

Isaiah 40:28____

Psalm 19:1-4____

Acts 14:17____

2. God is the Governor and Judge of the Moral Universe

The Bible portrays God as a moral Being. His outstanding attribute is holiness (Leviticus 19:2). He demands holiness in His people (1 Peter 1:16). Without holiness, no man will see the Lord (Hebrews 12:14). Mankind was created in God's image and thus he is a moral being. God endowed him with a rational mind, a free will, and a moral nature. God invested mankind with immense authority, giving him dominion over the entire animal kingdom (Genesis 1:28). He was placed in the Garden of Eden with instructions to cultivate it (Genesis 2:15). He was also told to be fruitful and multiply and replenish the earth (Genesis 1:28). In this way, God's rule and His love were to be extended throughout the earth.

Man was accountable only to God, his Maker. Unfortunately, man believed the lie of Satan that God was holding good back from him, and he disobeyed God. He was then alienated from God because he did not trust God and sinned. There are four broken conditions due to man's sin: a. Broken relationship with God, b. Broken relationship with self, c. Broken relationship with others, and d. Broken relationship with creation. Yet God was seeking to restore all of these relationships (Genesis 3:9). He is/was not willing that anyone should perish (2 Peter 3:9), but for all to come to a knowledge of the Truth, who is Jesus! (1 Timothy 2:4).

God prefers salvation to judgment. God's wrath makes the Cross of Jesus necessary. He so loved the world (John 3:16). This

Love is made so clear in the Old Testament in the actions of God towards the nation of Israel and the other nations.

3. God is the King and Ruler of the Gentile Nations

Because of the disobedience and arrogance of the human race, God confounded their language and thus scattered them over the face of the earth. God created the nations and they are the work of His hands (Psalms 86:9). The Dispersion of the nations described by Moses is an act of God and was arranged according to the number of the children of Israel (Deuteronomy 32:8).

Though the nations rejected God, they belonged to Him and were accountable to Him, whether or not they acknowledged that fact. The rule of God extends to all the world.

Psalm 103:19 ____________________________________

Psalm 24:1 ______________________________________

Psalm 47:2, 8 ____________________________________

God often used the heathen nations and their kings for His purposes. Cyrus was the King of a pagan nation (today's Iran or Persia). He had no clear knowledge of the one true God (Isaiah 45:4). Yet God used him as an instrument to accomplish His purpose for Israel. In this capacity, Cyrus is referred to as God's "shepherd" (Isaiah 44:28) and God's "anointed" (Isaiah 45:1).

4. God is the Father and Redeemer of Israel

Even though God's sovereign and universal dominion is over all the earth, the Old Testament tells the story of His dealings with one special people. This special people, Israel, is the instrument for the universal purpose of God for the salvation of the world.

Among all nations of the earth, Israel enjoyed a unique relationship to Jehovah God. All other nations were made by Him (Psalms 86:9) and ruled by Him (Psalms 103:19), but only Israel is said to have been "redeemed" by Him (Isaiah 43:1). Thirteen times, in the second half of Isaiah alone, Jehovah is referred to as the "Redeemer" of Israel.

Beginning with Genesis 12, history in the Old Testament is the history of Israel; and the history of Israel is the history of redemption. The call of Abraham marks a turning point in God's dealing with the world. Campbell Morgan divides the book of Genesis into three parts: Generation (1-2), Degeneration (3-11), and Regeneration (12-25). Abraham and Israel were not chosen by God for their own sake, but for the salvation of the whole world.

Genesis 12:3 ______________________________

Genesis 22:18 ______________________________

Genesis 28:14 ______________________________

John 4: 22______________________________

God had a threefold purpose in the election of Israel:

a. Israel was to be the recipient and the guardian of God's special revelation to the world (Hebrews 1:1-3)
b. Israel was to be the channel through which the Redeemer was to enter the stream of human history. He was to be the Son of Abraham (Matthew 1:1), of the tribe of Judah (Genesis 49:10), of the house of David (Romans 1:3).
c. Israel was to be God's servant (Isaiah 44:1-2), and witness (Isaiah 43:10) in the midst of the nations.

God chose Israel to be a "kingdom of priests and a holy nation" (Exodus 19:6, 1 Peter 2:9-10). God was passionate to use the people of Israel to declare His Name throughout all the nations (Exodus 9: 15-16, Romans 9). God dealt with his people in grace and judgment. In both ways, God used Israel as a witness to the nations (Psalms 67:1-2; Deuteronomy 28:1-14). Moreover, through the centuries, God has kept His promises. He warned all his potential enemies not to do any harm to His people (Psalms 105:15; Zechariah 2:8). Haman tried to hang them (Esther 3-7); Nebuchadnezzar tried to burn them (Daniel 3). In each case they proved to be indestructible. God, in His grace, intervened and delivered them from the hands of their enemies. In this way Israel became a witness to other nations of the saving power of Jehovah (Psalms 66:1-7; Isaiah 52:10). But, Israel did not always remain faithful. She was always surrounded by hostile Gentile nations whose political power posed a threat to Israel's sovereignty and whose pagan practices presented a temptation to commit idolatry. Yet she has not ceased to be God's witness. Israel by her presence, whether obedient or disobedient, was, and is, a witness to the one true God, Creator of heaven and earth and the Judge and Ruler of the world. In this passive way, she was fulfilling her "missionary" role.

Israel's Missionary Role Before the Captivity

Israel's salvation and blessings were not restricted to itself alone, but to the nations. As His covenant people, Israel was to remain separate from the Gentile nations. She was not to worship their gods (Deuteronomy 11:6), nor marry their children (Deuteronomy 7:30). At the same time, it was God's intention that she should be a "light to the nations" (Isaiah 42:6) in order that His salvation 'may reach to the end of the earth" (Isaiah 49:6). Prior to the Captivity, Israel's missionary activity was centripetal-an invitation to come and witness God's glory. The nations came to Israel, but she did not go out to them. The sole exception was Jonah's mission to Nineveh; and his message was one of judgment, not salvation. During this period, Israel's missionary activity developed into three stages.

1. "Strangers" were permitted to enter the Congregation of Israel

In the time of Solomon, the strangers numbered 153,600 (2 Chronicles 2:17) and were hired by Solomon in the building of the Temple. In some cases, restrictions were laid down. The Edomites had to wait until the third generation (Deuteronomy 23:7-8); others, such as the Ammonites and the Moabites, were not permitted to enter the congregation even to the tenth generation (Deuteronomy 23:3). Once the strangers were admitted into the congregation, they enjoyed considerable favor. They were permitted to keep the Passover (Numbers 9:14) and were required to observe the Sabbath (Exodus 20:10). They could even offer sacrifices (Leviticus 17:18). However, they could not become kings (Deuteronomy 17:15). Israel was given strict instructions not to oppress them (Exodus 22:21) and to treat them generously (Leviticus 19:9-10; 33-34).

The book of Ruth is a beautiful example of the way in which these strangers were assimilated into the congregation. Ruth, a Moabite widow, was not only accepted as a full member of the congregation, but she also became the grandmother of King David (Ruth 4:21-22) and ancestress of our Lord (Matthew 1:5). In the stories of Ruth and Rahab, we get a glimpse of the missionary concern of Israel even before the days of the prophets.

2. Entire nations were to be attracted to the God of Israel

Isaiah foresaw this (Isaiah 2:2-3). Jeremiah had this same emphasis (Jeremiah 3:17). The nations came to Israel's God; the people of Israel did not go to the nations. Israel, in the midst of the nations, served on their behalf as both priest and prophet. The vision conjured by Isaiah, who was another great prophet, depicted the Gentile nations making way to Jerusalem to hear the word of the Lord and to call on His name in prayer. Jerusalem was the only place on earth where they could do this.

3. All the nations would know and worship the Lord

A third stage in the development of Israel's missionary activities would be reached when a knowledge of the one true God would become universal. Habakkuk predicted it (Habakkuk 2:14). Other references for God's heart for all nations can be seen in Isaiah 1:11,11:9; Psalms 22:27, and Isaiah 49:6; 45:22.

Israel's Missionary Role During the Exile

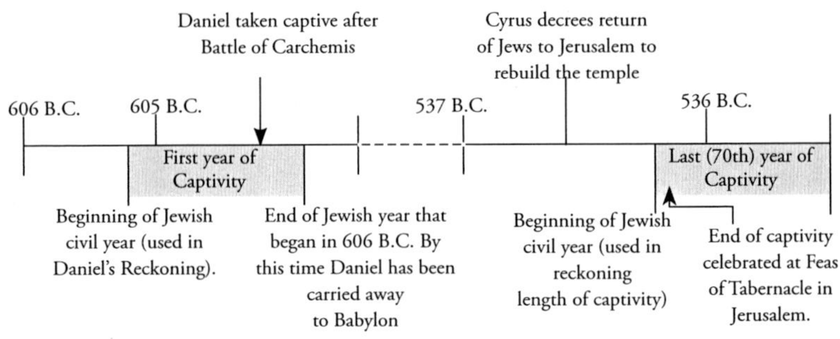

The captivity was God's judgment on Israel for her continued disobedience and lack of trust in, and love for, Him. Jerusalem was destroyed by Nebuchadnezzar, and the Jews were carried away captive to Babylon in approximately 600 B.C. After seventy years in captivity, only 42,000 people returned to Palestine under Governor Zerubbabel. The majority preferred to remain in exile, eventually representing about seven percent of the Roman Empire. These diaspora Jewish people continued a close contact with Jerusalem and their authorities. They sent generous offerings to maintain the Temple services (Acts 6:9). Every year the chief festivals attracted large numbers of Jews from all parts of the Mediterranean world (Acts 2:9-11). Wherever they went in the Greco-Roman world, they vigorously maintained the integrity of their religious faith, and thus were both admired and detested simultaneously.

It was during this period that Israel's missionary role completely changed and became centrifugal-go and proclaim God's glory. Instead of the nations flocking to Jerusalem to learn the law of the Lord, the law was taken by the Jews of the diaspora to the ends of the earth.

Six characteristics of Jewish religious life in the diaspora contributed directly to the making of converts and indirectly to the spread of Christianity later on.

a. The institution of the synagogue.
b. The observance of the Sabbath.
c. The translation of the Scriptures into Greek (Septuagint LXX).
d. The concept of monotheism (doctrine of one true God).
e. The practice of morality. Immorality and idolatry were two great sins of the pagan world. High moral standards of Judaism attracted the nations to the one true God.
f. The promise of the coming Savior. There was no genuine deliver in the Greco-Roman world. Into this vacuum stepped the Jews with their centuries-old expectation of a coming Messiah.

The Greco-Roman world listened and liked the message of Judaism. Thus, it became a missionary religion and helped prepare the way for Christian missions.

Questions for Discussion

1. Describe about the missionary heart of God in the Old Testament and outline key approaches of God towards the execution of His mission?
2. Who were the key instruments used for God's mission and elaborate their contribution?
3. Explain on the nature of God's mission in the Old Testament?
4. Mention and explain some of your key passages to describe the mission of God in the Old Testament?
5. What are the implications for the current Christian missions in India?

Chapter 3

Missions in the New Testament

In the New Testament, we see the coming of the Messiah - His birth, ministry, death, resurrection and ascension to heaven. It addresses how the mission of God was expanded through the power of the Holy Spirit, and teachings of the apostles, to allow them to live out and practice everywhere. "Sending" was the important principles in the Old Testament context of mission. It is much more central in the context of the New Testament. God sent his Son Jesus (John 20:21) and Jesus returns to God and sends the Holy Spirit to his followers (John 15:26; 16:7). They are sent by Jesus in the power of His Spirit, to declare the forgiveness of sins and the kingdom of God, and to live life bearing fruit unto God by His power and for His glory.

The New Testament is a missionary book in address, content, Spirit and design.[12] The New Testament does not limit theology to only reason and concept. It is theology in motion, the Word of God,

---

[12] A. Scott Moreau, Gary R. Corwin, Gary B. McGee, "Introducing World Missions: A Biblical, Historical, and Practical Survey (Grand Rapids: Baker publishing group, 2004), 40.

and it is true "missionary theology". It is "theo" (God) plus "-logy" (Logos or Word), and it reveals Jesus to us.

Missions in the Four Gospels

The New Testament clearly teaches a threefold purpose of the Incarnation of Jesus.[13]

1. To Reveal God, the Father

This comes out very clearly in John's Gospel (John 1:14, 18). This is even clearer in the words of Jesus Himself (John 14:6-7).

2. To Destroy the Work of the Devil

Natural man is not only a sinner in bondage to sin (Romans 7:14-20), but he is also a slave to Satan and captive in his kingdom of darkness (Matthew 12:25-29).

John 3:8 ____________________

Hebrew 2:14-15____________________

Colossians 2:13-15 ____________________

3. To Save the World, Not Just the Jewish People

He died for all people (John 3:16-17).

John 4:14 ____________________

2 Corinthians 5:14 ____________________

John 12:32 ____________________

Matthew 20:28____________________

Colossians 1:19 ____________________

Each of the four Gospels was written by a different author with a specific and unique purpose in mind. These different unique purposes reflect the missionary message of Christ to His Church.

---

[13] J. Herbert Kane, Christian Missions in Biblical Perspective (Grand Rapids: Baker House, 1976), 35-36.

I. The Gospel of Matthew

Matthew's main purpose is to confirm for his Jewish Christian audience that Jesus is their Messiah, the Savior, and the King of Kings. Matthew includes many proof texts (1:22-23; 2:15; 2:17-18; 2:23; 4:14-16; 8:17; 12:17-21; 13:35; 27:9-10).

Key Missiological verses in Matthew

Matthew 9:35-38 ________________________________

This passage reveals the compassion of Christ for the lost, and His methodology for reaching the harassed and helpless. His command has an urgency to pray and send out workers to the harvest field.

Matthew 24:14 ________________________________

In this passage, we see the heart of Christ for all people in the world. He cares about each person whether he or she are living in the cities or jungles. He came to save all peoples (*nations*) of the world.

Matthew 28:16-20 ________________________________

In this passage, we see the command of Christ not only to his disciples, but also to all believers, whether sent locally or globally. What is this command or Great Commission? To *go and make disciples* of all nations (*ethnolinguistic* groups in the world).

This passage has different elements:

All Authority - in heaven over angels, demons, Satan and any rulers or authorities in heavenly places. Also, He has authority on earth over kings, rulers, leaders and all people. The risen Jesus is completely qualified to direct and empower His disciples to go to the harvest fields.

The Foundational Command – is not to go, but to *make disciples* of all nations. What is a disciple? A disciple is one who is a learner, and who wants to be like the master or teacher. He is totally committed and surrendered to the message and lifestyle of his master. The central purpose of the church is to make true disciples of Christ for His glory through the power of His indwelling life. Disciples are the family of Jesus (Matthew 12:46-50), and they put Him ahead of all other earthly commitments (Matthew 8:21-22; Luke 14:26-27) to the extent that they are willing to suffer for the sake of the Gospel (Matthew 10:17-23).

Michael Wilkins expresses "what discipleship involves, and Jesus declared that to be a disciple is to become like the master (Matthew 10:24-25; Luke 6:40). Becoming like Jesus includes going out, through the power of the Holy Spirit, with the same message, ministry, and compassion (Matthew 10:5), practicing the same religious and social traditions (Matthew 12:1-8; Mark 2:18- 20), belonging to the same family of obedience (Matthew 12:46-49), exercising the same servanthood (Matthew 20:26-28; Mark 10:42-45; John 13:12-17), experiencing the same suffering (Matthew 10:16-25; Mark 10:38-39) and being sent in the same way to the same world (John 20:21)."[14]

How do we make disciples?

Evangelism - sharing the Good News (in a relevant way with love and humility).

Baptizing - in the name of the Triune God.

Teaching - everything that Christ has commanded.

---

[14] Michael Wilkins, "Following the Master: A Biblical Theology of Discipleship" (Zondervan Publishing House: Grand Rapids, Michigan), 174-194.

The purpose of teaching is to reveal Jesus in order to live in His grace, so that God's people will bear "much fruit" for His glory.

The Assurance of God's Presence, Promise and Power - Christ will be with you and me always, to the very end of the age. He is with His followers to protect, encourage and watch over them as they engage in the process of discipling others. He is our Good Shepherd.

Does Discipleship Include Justice?

Absolutely. The core of what Jesus taught is summarized in the command to love God and people (Matthew 19:16-26). "But Jesus radicalizes these commandments in a specific direction: To love one's neighbor means to have compassion on them...to see that justice is done. To become a disciple is to be incorporated into God's new community through baptism and to side with the poor and the oppressed..."[15]

II. The Gospel of Mark

The Gospel of Mark was written to Gentile Christians probably in the church at Rome. The purpose was to encourage the believers to persevere through suffering and persecution as they lived for Christ and spread His message. Mark presents Jesus as the Servant-Messiah and Son of God who died as a ransom for all sinners. Suffering

[15] David Bosch, "Transforming Mission: Paradigm Shifts in Theology of Mission" (New York: Orbis Books, 2006), 234-235.

for Him is part of Christ's mission. Jesus told us that we will be persecuted for His Name. See Mark 8:31, 34; 9:49; 13:9-13; 14:36.

Key Missiological verses in Mark

The calling of thedisciples (1:14-18) ____________________

Healing and spiritual warfare are elements of missions (Chapter 2-3)

____

The appointing of the twelve apostles (3:13-19) ____________________

Jesus sends out of the twelve (6:7-13) ____________________

Who is the greatest (9:33-37)____________________

Jesus' Purpose on earth (10:45)____________________

The Greatest Commandment (12:28-34) ____________________

Mission mandate (16:15-20)____________________

III. The Gospel of Luke

Luke was a Gentile physician and a missionary companion of Paul. Luke presents Jesus as the Messiah and Lord whose life, death and resurrection make salvation available to all people everywhere.

Key Missiological verses in Luke

The purpose of Jesus birth (Luke 1:26-33) ____________________

Jesus the Sent One (4:18-19)____________________

Kingdom life of disciples (6:20-49) ____________________

Jesus' ministry to all genders (7:36-50) ____________________

Jesus sends out the twelve (9:1-6) ____________________

The cost of following Jesus (9:57-62) ____________________

Jesus sends out the seventy-two (10:1-24) ____________________

The parable of the Lost Sheep, Lost Coin, Lost Son (15:1-32) ______________________________

Jesus the Sending One (24:46-48) ______________________

Jesus appears to the disciples (24:36-49) ______________________

Luke shows why Jesus was sent by His Father. He also shows the connection between Jesus' sending and ours. Christians are now the sent ones, with the explicit obligation to be witnesses to the life, death, and resurrection of Christ and to the need for repentance (i.e., turning to Jesus) for the forgiveness of sin, infilling of the Holy Spirit, and living by grace through faith. This message is to go to all nations by God's power. This is Christian mission.[16]

IV. The Gospel of John

John wrote primarily to non-Jewish believers and seeking unbelievers. He presents Jesus as the Word, the Messiah and the incarnate of Son of God, who has come to reveal the Father and to bring eternal life to all who believe in Him. In this Gospel, God is the center of mission. It is He who so loved the world that He sent His unique son (3:16). This book is an evangelistic one; throughout this book we see great emphasis on missions. Jesus is the focus of the message.

Key Missiological verses in John about Jesus

He is the Sent One (1:1) ______________________

He came from the Father (1:18) ______________________

He does what He was sent to do (5:36) ______________________

He glorifies God (1:14; 13:31-32) ______________________

He sends those who follows Him (20:21) ______________________

[16] A. Scott Moreau, Gary R. Corwin, and Gary B. McGee, *Introducing World Missions: A Biblical, Historical, and Practical Survey* (Grand Rapids: Baker publishing group, 2004), 49.

John's Gospel is rich in the vocabulary of *send* - the term and its derivatives appear almost sixty times in twenty chapters. A quick look at the passages shows that John's perspective on why Jesus was sent is clear: to save the world (3:17); to do God's will (4:34); to finish God' work (5:36; 9:4), which includes believing in the One whom God sent (6:29); to work for the honor of the One who sent Him (7:18); to tell what He heard from God to the whole world (8:26; 12:47-50) and in this way make God and His love known to the world (17:25-26).[17] Our task is to receive Him into our hearts by faith, knowing this is a gift, and then, through His indwelling life in us, we learn to trust and obey Him and declare His works. We can then bring the lost to Him by sharing God's heart, and then disciple them so that they can bear fruit and glorify God through the power of His indwelling Holy Spirit working through us, living not by rules and regulations under the law, but under grace through faith in Him.

Questions for Discussion

1. Explain Jesus' person and ministry in the light of God's mission in the New Testament?
2. What is the nature of God's mission found in the New Testament?
3. How does the Great Commission of our Lord Jesus Christ applies to the current mission scenario?
4. Who are the key proponents of God's mission in the New Testament and mention briefly about their contribution?
5. What are the challenges in India to accomplish the Great Commission and how to overcome those?

---

[17] Moreau, Corwin and McGee, *Introducing World Missions*, 49.

Chapter 4

Missions in the Acts of the Apostles

The Gentile physician Luke authored the Acts of Apostles. He was a missionary companion of Paul. It is a continuation of the Gospel of Luke. Luke addressed to a man named Theophilus, but it was intended for all the believers. Luke shows how the Gospel rapidly spread from Jerusalem to the whole Roman empire and from its Jewish roots to the Gentile world.

The main purposes of the book appear to be:

a. To present a detailed history of the Christian church including its origin, the spread of the Gospel, the establishment of congregations, and evangelistic efforts.
b. To give a defense of the gospel with the goal of winning Jews and Gentiles to Christ.
c. To provide a guide for the generations to follow for building Jesus's kingdom here on earth.
d. To depict the triumph of the gospel in the face of bitter persecution. This book demonstrates how the church triumphed under the rule of the exalted Christ and

through the power of the Holy Spirit in the midst of severe persecution.

The key verse in Acts is 1:8 ____________________________

The book is divided into three clearly defined parts as it traces the expansion of the gospel beginning with Jerusalem (1-7), progressing to Judea and Samaria (8-12), and then extending ultimately to the ends of the earth (13-28).

Graham Scroggie in his book, *Know Your Bible,* finds four important concepts in Acts 1:8:

a. The central theme of the Christian witness is Christ.
b. The exclusive medium of the witness is the church.
c. The ultimate scope of the Christian witness is the world.
d. The unfailing secret of the Christian witness is the Holy Spirit.[18]

The Works of the Apostles

The book of Acts records the ministry of the apostles in the early church. Ordinary people became powerful and extraordinary in the hands of God through His Spirit for the expansion of His church.

The disciples became full-fledged apostles to represent Christ and the building of His church. They were transformed through various dramatic events such as the resurrection, the ascension, and the Pentecost. They were empowered for a worldwide ministry.

There was radical transformation in the disciples in their ministry approach and attitude. They received new insight into the Scripture (Acts 2:25-31), and a new initiative for action amid controversies/complaints (Acts 8:14-25; Chapter 15). They had a new power in their ministry service. They were given power to heal the sick and cast out demons (Matthew 10:1). They received a new courage in witnessing (John 20:19; Acts 4:19-20; 5:29). They had such a boldness to preach the Word without fear (Acts 4:29).

---

[18] J. Herbert Kane, "Christian Missions in Biblical Perspective," (Grand Rapids: Baker House, 1976), 51.

The Content of the Apostles' Witness

The apostles were physically with Jesus and thus they were eyewitness of the works of Christ, especially the Resurrection (1 Corinthians 9:1; Acts 1:22). Both Peter and John argued that their association with Christ made it possible for them to speak with integrity and authority (2 Peter 1:16-18; John 1:1-3).

The witness of the apostles revolved around a central theme which is Jesus Christ.

Acts 2:32 - Peter at Pentecost ______________________

8:5 - Philip went down to the city of Samaria ______________

8:35 - Phillip to the Ethiopian eunuch __________________

In 2 Corinthians 4:5, Paul summed it all up when he said: "For what we preach is not ourselves, but Jesus Christ the Lord."

The apostles witness included four important truths regarding Christ.

1. The Identify of His Person

Even though Jesus presented himself as a Messiah to the Jews, they rejected Him and His offer of the Kingdom because they expected a different kind of Messiah. The apostles who were the eyewitness of Jesus' life did not lose heart, instead they continued to preach the truth that Jesus was the Christ. They based their approach on two considerations: the prophecies of the Old Testament and the mighty works that accompanied Jesus' ministry (Luke 24:25-27; Acts 3:18; 13:29; 17:2-3; 4:27-28; John 10:24-25; Acts 2:22-23; Luke 24:19; Isaiah 35:4-6).

2. The Nature of His Death

The apostles preached boldly that by the death of Christ, the shedding of His blood, our sins are forgiven. The Jews knew very well that "without the shedding of blood there is no forgiveness of sins" (Hebrew 9:22).

1 Peter 1:18-20 ____________________________

John 6:55 ____

Hebrew 9:26 ____

1 Corinthians 15:3 ________________________________

1 Corinthians 5:7 _________________________________

1 Peter 3:18 _______________________________________

Peter 2:24 ____

Corinthians 5:21 ___________________________________

3. The Truth of the Resurrection

Paul says: "If Christ has not been raised, your faith is futile, and you are still in your sins" (1 Corinthians 15:17). Wherever the apostles went, they preached "Jesus and the Resurrection." They preached it to the Jews in Jerusalem (Acts 4:2), the Gentiles in Caesarea (Acts 10:40), and the philosophers in Athens (Acts 17:31). It was the central issue in Paul's defense before Felix (Acts 24:15, 21), Festus (25:19), and Agrippa (26:8, 23). To know Christ and the power of His resurrection was their highest ambition (Philippians 3:10). To preach the unsearchable riches of Christ to Jew and Gentile was the greatest of all privileges (Ephesians 3:7-10). By His law of love, they were determined to live (2 Corinthians 5:14-15), and for His name they were prepared to die (Acts 21:13).[19]

4. The Hope of His Return

Jesus told his disciples that He will come again (John 14:3), and the angels confirmed this promise (Acts 1:1). God's plan for the restoration of all things, summed up by Jesus in the concept of the kingdom of God, was not denied or delayed by the unbelief of the Jews or by the gathering in of the Gentiles. Jesus Christ will come again, with power and glory (Luke 21:27), to rapture the church (1 Thessalonians 4:14-18), to execute judgment (2 Thessalonians 1:4-10), and to establish His kingdom (Matthew 25:31-46). Paul,

---

[19] Kane, "Christian Missions in Biblical Perspective," 59.

in his preaching to the philosophers in Athens, warned that Jesus is coming to judge the world in righteousness... (Acts 17:30-31).[20]

5. The Nature of the Witness

The apostles' witness was effective and powerful. They gave their testimony to the resurrection of the Lord Jesus, and great grace was upon them all (Acts 4:33). The Apostolic witness was verbal (Acts 8:4, 25, 40, 9:20; 2 Timothy 4:2; 1 Corinthians 9:16), visible - saw then listened (Acts 8:6), and vital (Matthew 7:28-29). Common people were attracted to Jesus because of the vitality of His teaching.

2 Corinthians 6:8-10 ______________________________

Acts 17:6 ______________________________

Questions for Discussion

1. According to Acts 1:8, what were the prerequisites for the disciples to enter into ministry?
2. Mention the major characters from the Acts of Apostles and their contribution for the tremendous expansion of ministries?
3. Elaborate on the inception of the church and mention few unique aspects of early church?
4. How do you understand the significance of persecution in the early Christianity?
5. Prepare a check-list of growth parameters for your respective churches based on the principles found in the Acts of the Apostles.

[20] Kane, "Christian Missions in Biblical Perspective," 60.

Chapter 5

Understanding Holistic Mission

Introduction

The term "holistic" is widely used not only in the Christian mission, but also adapted in the secular approaches. Due to its wider scope and sustainable long-term impact, several initiatives have been taken to implement this model to improve overall results. Both "integral" mission and "holistic" mission is interchangeably used to accomplish the same purpose.

Defining the Terminology

The root meaning of the term holistic implies 'whole' derived from the Greek origin ***holos.*** The very meaning of the term holistic entails the transformational impact of the Gospel in all dimensions of an individual or a community of people. One of the papers presented at the Christian Conference of Asia succinctly defines the holistic mission in the challenging context of Asia. It presents the primary objectives of holistic mission in four dimensions.[21]

[21] Cung Lian Hup, Holistic Mission in the Context of Asia, http://cca.org.hk/home/page 6 (only this information available).

a. Attending to the needs of the total person.
b. Affirming the divine image within them.
c. Opposing the forces that distort that divine image.
d. Assisting the flowering or blooming of that divine image into its fullness.

The God of the Bible is passionate and proactive to restore the broken relationship with fallen humankind. The process of transformation and restoration begins with our understanding and acknowledgement of the *imago Dei* (image of God) and purpose for every individual. As the salt and light, the called-out people of God are born of God again and by the indwelling Spirit they are given their role in restoring the totality of an individual or community through the proclamation and living out of the Gospel. The Lausanne Covenant states, "The Whole Church taking the Whole Gospel to the Whole World". The 'Whole Church' is irrespective of ethnic, lingual, cultural and denominational diversities mandated to carry out the mission of God. Unless we deliberately choose to overcome our differences by acknowledging and celebrating our diversities, the church will be incapable of understanding God's grand purpose. The 'Whole Gospel' always addresses all spheres of human life without neglecting any. This means that spiritual, social, emotional, economic, etc. needs are equal beneficiaries of complete restoration through God's love and grace. Finally, holistic mission is meant for 'The Whole World'. The entirety of humankind in all its aspects is the key concern of the heart of God and needs God's transformation.

At the outset, holistic mission is widely comprised of the proclamation of the Good News (i.e., that Jesus died, rose, and we are now in Him as believers), the ongoing discipleship at the local level, the building of Christ-centered communities of disciples through the gatherings of the called ones, the living out of the Gospel through the practical demonstration of compassion and love, the understanding and resisting of the elements of societal injustice to preserve the divine dignity of others, and the accountable and faithful ownership of God-given resources.

Biblical Foundation for Holistic Missions

The creation account mentioned in the first two chapters of Genesis lays the foundation for the background for holistic mission. This account not only introduces God as the Only Creator but also enlightens us about the purpose behind His creation. He beautifully orchestrated the order of creation so that there would not be any chaos. As the peak of His creation, and His finest handiwork, God created Adam. God blessed Adam with Eve, the helper who would accompany Him. After the completion of all creation, they were bestowed with authority and ownership under God's Lordship and declared excellent. (Genesis 1:28-31). More importantly, they had the privilege to have direct access to God's fellowship and constant communion.

This creation account is not just a story of something that came into existence on its own. In addition, it is not just a story of two mere human beings without any purpose to contribute. So, what does the creation account contribute to the concept of holistic mission? As we delve more into understanding the God of creation and His love, the more we will explore His divine purposes for humankind. It becomes essential to recognize the fact that *Missio Dei* overflows from thevery being and character of God.

The first chapter in Genesis presents the God of excellence and creativity who would intelligently bring creation into existence. The self-existent God now makes His presence evident through creation. In addition to that, He chooses to create man in His own image, sharing the likeness and attributes. Moreover, he proves His love and generosity by making required provision, entrusting the entire creation to the care of the man, and blessing him with constant fellowship.

Therefore, the God of creation is the Intelligent One, Compassionate, Relational, Mindful, Communicator, Provider, Holistic, and more importantly Purposeful. God always desired to maintain fellowship, harmony and beauty in creation. Adam and Eve were created with a holistic blessing that would always keep them alive for the purpose of continuing to reflect God's nature and rule over all creation diligently, under His Lordship and Love. Thus, creation reflected the qualities and attributes of God.

The Consequences of the fall of Man[22]

The denial of God's Lordship, and the lack of trust in God's love, invokes distortion to the very purpose of God for our lives. Adam and Eve did this as they each independently choose to explore life beyond the God designed frame for them. They believed the lie of Satan that God was withholding something good from them, and so they did not trust Him. What were the immediate effects of their disobedience?

a. They fell into the trap of the devil by doubting God's love and denying His lordship.
b. They distorted their self-worth of being created in the image of God, which led them to withdraw themselves with a sense of guilt and shame. Their distrust and disobedience distorted their realization of their God-created wholeness and attributed divine likeness.
c. The everlasting and constant fellowship and communion with God was breached. They no longer had confidence to walk with God.
d. They fell short of the purpose of taking ownership over all creation. In fact, they became dependent on the creation for their continuous existence. They now had to work the ground to survive.
e. Although, they were physically alive, their spiritual death caused them to be driven out of the Garden of Eden, which had been the beautiful provision of God for them.
f. There came a curse on Eve, who had to endure pain to give birth, along with a curse that would open ways for other physical illness.
g. The companionship intended for Adam and Eve was greatly affected by their disobedience. Even though Adam and Eve were equally created in the image of God, the

[22] J. N. Manokaran, "Christ and Transformational Missions," (Chennai: Mission Educational Books, 2008), 288.

curse made Adam desire to become Eve's master instead of her leader. Instead of companionship, they are cursed with trying to exercise power over each other.

h. Even the land was cursed. Scripture testifies that all creation is groaning for our salvation. The act of disobedience to God's intended purposes created universal damage in all dimensions of human life. The consequences resulted in a universal catastrophe. The wholeness created by God was intensely disturbed and this acts as the background for the intervention of God to bring restoration of the fallen humankind and creation. Since then, God has been approaching humankind with the message of love, peace, restoration and reconciliation by sending priests, kings, judges, prophets and different personalities to accomplish his divine mission of bringing back His people. In the entire Old Testament, we find God involved in multi-dimensional or holistic approaches to redeem His people. He showed significant interest in the political affairs of that time. He became the voice for the oppressed and voiceless by ensuring justice. His compassion for the gentile nation is worth noting.

In the fullness of time (Galatians 4:4), His love for His creation was so immense that He choose to send His only son Jesus Christ as the ultimate solution to universal sin and its consequences. Jesus's death and resurrection paved the way for us to reconcile with God and they have given us the ability, through faith and grace, to regain the wholeness that was always intended for us. We become children of God, heirs with Christ, and we have His Life in Him. We are already seated with Him in heavenly places, and we are truly born again as sons and daughters of God, our Father.

Discovering Jesus' Holistic Approach to Mission[23]

Jesus's life and ministry in the New Testament are critical models for holistic mission. Even though He lived for only three and a half

[23] Manokaran, "Christ and Transformational Missions," 288-289.

years, the impact of His ministry has affected all human history. Jesus ministered to all the needs of humankind (physical, mental, emotional, spiritual, etc.) and He made the Good News a reality in their lives. The following characteristics of Jesus's holistic mission must be incorporated and realized in modern Christian missions.

1. Incarnational

One of the profound characteristics of our Lord Jesus Christ' holistic ministry, was his ability to incarnate into the multi-context of humankind. Incarnation is defined herein as the translation of oneself into a cultural or societal context. Through His incarnation, Jesus distinctively entered into the context of that time, but He was unaffected by the fallen sin nature of humankind. He associated with sinners but in Him was found no sin, He knew no sin, and He did no sin, yet He became sin for us at the cross. He was born into the Jewish culture, but His entire life and ministry always exceeded the standards and practices of that culture. John the apostle highlights Jesus Christ as the perfect embodiment of God bringing forgiveness, truth and life, and who became flesh (human) and dwelt among us. Jesus's incarnational approach to fallen humankind fulfilled and satisfied God's just demands and made salvation possible. Without His incarnation, we would never be able to come into God's presence as His children and witness the glory of our Heavenly Father God.
As we partner with God in carrying out His holistic mission on earth, we do not become another Jesus. However, when we shine forth the likeness of Jesus through our lives and ministry, by the outworking of the gifts He puts in us through His Holy Spirt indwelling us, we translate ourselves into the context of Christian missions and are kept by His grace from being diluted by the world's sinful nature. The Holy Spirit convicts the world of sin; He does not convict believers of sin, but rather, of righteousness.

John 16:8 ____

John 1:14 ____

2. Purpose Driven

The four gospels in the New Testament strongly emphasize Jesus's definite and deep acknowledgement of the purpose for which He incarnated as a human being. His entire ministry emerged and was driven by a divine purpose. He Himself mentioned the purpose for which he was sent in several Scriptural passages. It was the recognition of His purpose that kept Him away from fulfilling the false expectations of the people around him. He withdrew himself from the benefits of popularity that had the potential to divert Him from His purpose. With His last breath on the cross, as He declared "It is finished", He announced the completion of His earthly purpose and His utter dedication and commitment to the divine purpose.

A Christian mission originated, guided and guarded with divine purpose can produce unprecedented and multi-dimensional blessings to accommodate all the needs of humankind.

John 4:34 ________________________________

Matthew 9:12-13 ________________________________

Luke 4:18-19 ________________________________

John 10:10-11 ________________________________

John 17:4 ________________________________

3. Inclusivity

Being renowned as one of the monotheistic faiths among existing religions of the world, Christian faith stands unique because of its many exclusive claims. Noteworthy are the seven great "I am sayings" proclaimed by Jesus which highlight Christianity's uniqueness. On the other hand, the Jesus who claims to be the only Way, Truth and Light (John 14:6), executes His mission in a manner that includes all mankind. Therefore, Jesus was exclusive by his divine position, but inclusive in fulfilling the divine purpose. Hence, we find people from many different backgrounds, tribes and social status included as the core disciples. It was a team of multi-cultural, multi-linguistic and multi-ethnic people that made up the early church.

The characteristic of inclusiveness in Jesus's mission surpassed all ethnic, geographical, philosophical, and social boundaries of that time. In like manner, as Christian missionaries around the world outwork His Life in them, and accomplish His work through His grace and favor, they need to rise above ethnic, lingual, national, racial, and other differences and walk worthy of Jesus in a manner that achieves Christ-centered holistic mission.

4. Demonstration of Love through Service

God's love has always been demonstrational from the beginning of the creation. Being a loving God, the Father always found ways to express His joy, fellowship and purpose intended for humankind. But, the fall of Adam and Eve brought a separation between humankind and God, and there was not a good way for God to fully express His love for His people until Jesus came. The highest expression of God's love for the world was manifested in His sending His only Son Jesus Christ into the world. The unconditional love of God is the essential element in God's mission and is incarnated in the life and ministry of our Lord and Savior Jesus Christ. And it is when we express His love as a fruit of the Spirit in our lives as our means and motivation of our services to humanity, that we make a true and lasting difference in the world around us.

Jesus's exceedingly deep love for humanity was revealed in the compassion He showed when He encountered needy people. He never judged those who approached him with needs, even though there was sin in their lives, but He welcomed, healed and helped everyone who came to Him by faith. Jesus, as the Son of Man, commended a group of righteous people who did not judge others but who understood the essence of mission and demonstrated it through the act of loving service to the neediest. In contrast, Jesus also talked of a group of judgmental people who claimed to know Him but never demonstrated it through practical service to others. Are these examples not a wake-up call for Christian missions that claim to exist for God's service but which do not demonstrate God's purposes through loving care and service to others? How are you choosing to express your commitment to the Lord and His mission?

John 3:16 ______________________________

Matthew 25:31-46 ______________________________

5. Scripturally Authenticated

The foundation for Jesus' holistic approaches to ministry was based on the Scripture. His earthly life and ministry was a fulfillment of everything that was written in the Scripture. Not even once in His entire life on earth did Jesus contradict the Word of God. Jesus said He did not come to abolish but fulfill to the law. In the Nazareth manifesto, we find Jesus introducing this purpose of His ministry. Jesus was completely mindful of the fact that His multi-dimensional, holistic mission was based totally on the Word of God. In fact, He Himself is the living Word of God made flesh. The authenticity and purpose for a holistic ministry are dependent on its intentional rooting in Scripture. Any Christian mission that aligns itself with, and finds its purpose for existence in, the Scripture, is aligning itself with the heart of God. The entire Bible depicts God's love for humankind and His tireless missional approach to reestablish a lost relationship. Our reliable and faithful adherence to the Scriptures will ensure authenticity in our holistic involvement in mission.

Matthew 5:17 ______________________________

Isaiah 61:1-2 ______________________________

Luke 4:16-21 ______________________________

6. Kingdom-Centered

Jesus' entire ministry centered around the central theme of the Kingdom of God. The *Zondervan* Pictorial Encyclopedia of the Bible says, "The word 'kingdom' is found fifty-five times in Matthew; twenty times in Mark, forty-six times in Luke and five times in John. When allowance is made for the use of the word to refer to secular kingdoms and for parallel verses of the same sayings of Jesus, the phrase 'the kingdom of God' and equivalent expressions (e.g., 'Kingdom of heaven,' 'his kingdom') occurs about eighty times. These statistics show the great importance of the concept in the teachings of Jesus. There can, therefore, be little doubt that the phrase 'the kingdom of God' expresses the main theme of His teaching."[24]

Matthew 19:13-14 ______________________________

Matthew 21:28-32 ______________________________

Matthew 6:31-33 ______________________________

John 3:3-7 ______________________________

Questions for Discussion

1. How do you perceive holistic mission?
2. What are the significance of holistic mission in the context of India?
3. What are the challenges for holistic mission in India?
4. Why do you think that Jesus' ministries were holistic in nature?
5. How can your local church engage in the holistic ministries?

---

[24] Merrill C. Tenney, *Zondervan Pictorial Encyclopedia*, (Grand Rapids: Zondervan, 1976), 804.

Chapter 6

Church and Christian Missions

God has been actively involved in redeeming the fallen creation and in reconciling it to Himself to display and reveal His Lordship and His love for it. Many individuals have become His divine instruments to carry out these purposes. Together, they form the church, which is one of the mysteries hidden since the foundation of the world (Ephesians 3:9, Colossians 1:26) and which helps accomplish the mission of God. One of the main reasons of the church's existence, call, and purpose is to facilitate the formation of the Kingdom of God by developing Christians to be the salt and light of the world. This chapter will assist the reader with understanding the historical background and biblical basis of "church" by exploring its God-given identity and divine purpose.

Terminology

The New Testament provides a clear picture of what is the "Church" and how it should function. It derives from the Greek word "*Ekklesia*" which is a combination of two Greek words i.e., *kaleo* which means "to call" and *ek* which means "out of."[25] Hence, the Church is the people of God who are called out of the world. The word "church" implies that we are called out by God for a specific purpose, which is to accomplish His mission of spreading the Gospel as the chosen people of God.

Acts 7:38 ____

Acts 19:32 ____

Hebrew 2:12 ____

Mathew 16:18 ____

Acts 19:41 ____

The diverse ranges of meaning and concept of *ekklesia* are being used throughout the New Testament. Some other dominant implied meanings which can be found in the scripture are fellowship, worship and service in the context of local congregation.

The Biblical Metaphors for Church

Generally, metaphors are used as figurative terms to compare or represent something. In the Bible, metaphors are used to unravel the enigmatic truths of God to enhance understanding. While several minor metaphors are used in the Bible, only the major metaphors are presented below. The metaphors that are used for the church convey its nature and function, ultimately aimed at the fulfillment of God's purposes. They also convey the Biblical rootedness of the church without which its existence cannot be explained.

1. The Body of Christ

One of the most important aspects of the High Priestly prayer of Jesus before His crucifixion on the cross was the "prayer for unity". During His life and ministry, Jesus knew that the potential threat for the church would come not from without but from within in the form of disunity. The reality of the problem of disunity is explained

---

[25] Peters George W, *A Biblical Theology of Missions* (Chicago: Moody Press, 1988), 200.

when the church is descriptively and figuratively called the Body of Christ. The Body of Christ, or the church, is comprised of people of diverse races, colors, ethnicities, languages and other characteristics. In spite of this diversity, however, the church is considered in the Bible to be one body. The metaphor of the Body of Christ presents Jesus as the Head and all other organs or parts of the body as the community of believers. Being the Head of the Church, Jesus has the Headship or Lordship over all members.

As members of the Body of Christ, we reverence Jesus, our Lord, by promoting unity rather than disunity. Any conflict in the church due to lack of unity is a direct affront to the authority of Christ who is the head of the church. One who causes conflict among others in the church invites self-damage to the Body of Christ as a whole. Because India is a very diverse country in terms of culture, languages, religions, etc., Indian churches must return to their Biblical foundation and honor the Lordship of Christ by promoting unity among the believers.

Ephesians 1:22-23 ______________________________

1 Corinthians 12:27 ______________________________

Romans 12:5 ______________________________

Ephesians 4:12 ______________________________

Ephesians 4:6 ______________________________

2. The Temple of God

This metaphor has been used to describe the relationship between God and His people. The Book of Exodus in the Old Testament recounts God's presence with His people in a pillar of fire and smoke. Later, the tabernacle and the temple in Jerusalem became dwelling places for God where He blessed His people with His divine presence. In the New Testament, we have the new covenant and Jesus, who physically tabernacled Himself and dwelt among us. Today, post Ascension of Jesus into heaven, The New Testament calls every believer a temple of God because of the indwelling of the Holy Spirit and Christ in us, the hope of glory. As people of the new covenant, we are privileged to be the custodians of God's presence in us; and because we have been made righteous through Jesus's death on the cross, His presence will never depart from us. We have this treasure in earthen vessels, and we love, honor and revere Him in our entire being.

1 Corinthians 3:9-15 ______________________________

Ephesians 2: 20-22______________________________

Peter 2:5______________________________

3. The Bride of Christ

The metaphor of the church as Christ's bride is an analogy which compares the relationship between a husband and wife to Christ and His church. This metaphor expresses the nobility and depth of Jesus's love for His church. It also beautifully suggests an elevation of the position of the church since it is **His** bride.[26] Christ the bridegroom has chosen the church to be His bride. As in customs of marriage in ancient times the bride, i.e., the church, is separated from the bridegroom, i.e. Christ, for a period of time until they are united at the wedding. During this period of separation, there is loving anticipation for each other. The bridegroom wants his bride to be holy and without blemish when they unite, so Jesus keeps us holy and blameless through His grace until His return. Sin does not have dominion over us, because we are not under the law, which He fulfilled for us, but we are under grace.

As the community of called out believers, we are chosen by God to love and serve Him. Because of His sacrificial love for us, the church is kept close to Him in His very heart. Because of His great love we are constantly cleansed by His Blood and are empowered by the Holy Spirit to remain holy and faithful as individuals and as a church.

Ephesians 5:2,25 ______________________________

Corinthians 11:2 ______________________________

[26] Earl D. Radmacher, *What the Church is all About: A Biblical and Historical Study* (Chicago: Moody Press, 1978), 256-265.

Ephesians 5:24 ______________________________

Revelation 19:7-9 ______________________________

Revelation 21:1-2 ______________________________

4. The Family of God

The Bible portrays the church as the family of God and the household of God. It is not portrayed in the Scriptures as a mere institution, completely regulated by a set of rules and regulations. God wants his family in the church to joyfully fulfill his calling and purpose through His power in grace. A horizontal aspect of Christian life in the church is comprised of the relationships developed among believers. The principal characteristic of these relationships is familial love. Jesus often used the metaphor of family to explain his relationship with His (and our) Heavenly Father, and Paul used this metaphor in his writings as well. Many other authors of books of the Bible, as led by the Spirit, incorporated the concept of the family of God to convey God's heart.

"A vertical aspect of Christian life, i.e., the relationship between God and believers in the church, is denoted by the familial language and terms used in the Bible. The Book of 1 John uses sibling language 14 times, James 12, and Hebrews 8. 1 John also uses "father" 12 times, "child" 17 times, and "son" 22 times. Hebrews also use "son" 12 times and "child" 3 times.[27]

Key Verses:

1 Timothy 5:1-2 ______________________________

Ephesians 3:14 ______________________________

Hebrews 2:11-12 ______________________________

Galatians 3:26-27 ______________________________

Ephesians 2:19 ______________________________

1 John 4:7 ______________________________

---

[27] Kruse Kronicle. https://www.krusekronicle.com/kruse_kronicle/archives.html#.XQh76IgzbDd.

5. The Royal Priesthood

The royal priesthood of each believer is a crucial paradigm shift in the New Testament from the Old Testament. The priesthood in the Old Testament was limited only to the tribe of Levi and the presence of God was not accessible to all. Through the sacrificial death of our Lord Jesus Christ, all those believe in Him are forever saved and become kings and priests unto God. Our access to his holy Presence is never impeded, even by sin, since we always stand before Him in the righteousness of Christ, our Savior (1 John 1:9).

Being the royal priesthood, believers in the church must intercede on behalf of fallen humankind in the world. Believers in the church must recognize the necessity of standing in the gap and crying out for the nations. There may be a tendency for individuals in the church to take selfish pride in their priestly function at the expense of humbly beseeching the Lord, and to misuse their divine callings to promote their own agendas. We must remind ourselves that we are called to impact the world as salt and light and with His tender love.

1 Peter 2:9-10 ____

Exodus 19:5-6 ____

Revelation 1:6 ____

Isaiah 61:6 ____

6. The Church as the Temple of the Holy Spirit

In Acts 2, the Holy Spirit was actively involved in safeguarding and sustaining the church. Believers were infilled with His power on the Day of Pentecost and were given the power to preach the Gospel, the Good News of Jesus. The New Testament imagery that most closely approximates or metaphors the relationship between the believer and the Holy Spirit is that of "temple" or "house" since the Holy Spirit indwells us, giving Christ's life from within. The Holy Spirit so enlivens us and the church community that His life in us becomes the herald of, and the instrument for, the eventual transformation of the whole cosmos "for which all creation groans."[28]

Key Verses:

Ephesians 2:21-22 ________________________________

1 Peter 2:5 ____________________________________

Acts 1:8 ______________________________________

Ephesians 4:1-3 ________________________________

The above metaphors of the church as the Body of Christ, the Temple of God, the Bride of Christ, the Royal Priesthood, the Family of God, and the Temple of the Holy Spirit, reveal to us the intended purposes of God for His church. Essentially, the church is God's perfect plan to accomplish His goal to reconcile the fallen world with Himself through His Son, by the power of the Holy Spirit.

The Church and Mission Relationship[29]

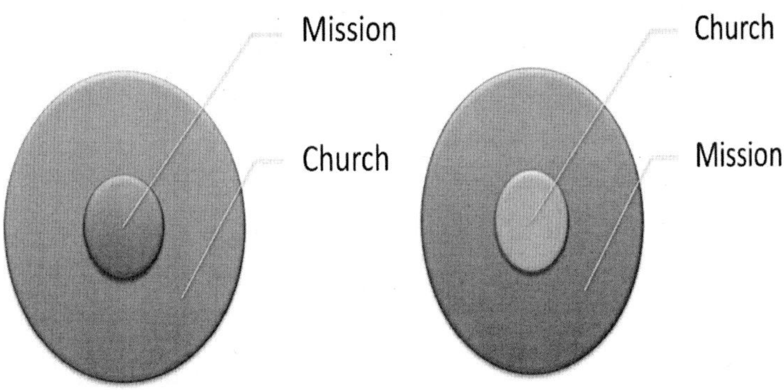

In today's Christendom, we witness the discouraging fact that some Christians in the church do not seem to understand the

[28] Nature and Mission of the church: A Stage on the way to a common statement, WCC publication, Faith and order paper 198, Geneva, p 8. (https://ecumenism.net/archive/wcc/2005_wcc_fo_nature_mission_church_en.pdf).

[29] Image taken fromhttps://upper-register.typepad.com/blog/2012/09/how-do-church-and-mission- relate.html, dated 7th, Feb, 2019.

purpose for their existence in the world and hence, churches do not contribute faithfully to the mission of God on earth, i.e., to bring all mankind to Jesus. There is a distinct demarcation and division between the entities of "church" and "mission". We ask:

Did the church emerge from and for God's mission to redeem fallen humankind and to show Satan God's heart for mankind which was planned from the foundation of the world? (Ephesians 3:9).

OR

With the church being a separate entity, is "mission" only one of several reasons that church exists? This debate somehow portrays "church "and "mission" as completely different from one another. However, authors like Tim Keller suggest that "a 'missional' church focuses every single part of its total life—its worship, community, public discourse, preaching, teaching, etc.—for the express purpose of winning non-believers to Christ from the non-Christian culture surrounding it."[30] I personally believe that the church, as the called out people of God, has emerged from the missionary heart of God Who wants to reach out to His creation. The church's existence, testimony and missional engagement in the world reflects the intensity with which our Heavenly Father is trying to build His earthly kingdom of believers in His Son Jesus and the finished work of His death and resurrection through the power of His Holy Spirit indwelling believers. A denial or lack of response to this reality of the true mission of God is a denial of God's love and purposes.

Three-Dimensional Missional Relationship of Church

George Peters correctly asserts that, "from the teaching of the New Testament, it is easily perceived that the church operates in three relationships: upward to God in worship and glorification; inward to herself in edification, purification, education and discipline; and outward to the world in evangelization and service ministries."[31] These three dimensions or relationships are so interlinked that one

---

[30] Tim Keller, "Contextual and Missional," .Lecture Three of the Urban Plant Life series of the London Church Planting Consultation, 2008-2009, p. 1.

[31] Peters George W, *A Biblical Theology of Missions* (Chicago: Moody Press, 1988), 209.

cannot be executed without the other. The church must recognize these dimensions of her relationship with the Lord in order to fulfill its mission.

1. The Upward Relationship

One purpose of existence of the church is to glorify God by making Him known to all the ends of the earth. The fulfillment of this divine purpose succeeds with the recognition of our upward relationship with God. Any church which is not rooted in relationship with God will ultimately lose the essence of God's purposes. Churches' superficial communication with God without the proper communion with Him will lack the disclosure of divine mysteries of God. The church itself is one of the mysteries of God (Ephesians 3:9, Colossians 1:26), hidden from the fallen angels since the foundation of the world. The upward relationship with God enables the church to focus on Jesus Christ and proclaim His sacrificial love and eternal purposes for all of mankind. As His bride, the church is called to an intimate spiritual and loving relationship with Jesus.

Isaiah 54:5 ______________________________

Ezekiel 16 ______________________________

Ephesians 5:21-33 ______________________________

2. The Inward Relationship

When growing in their inward relationship with God, Christians in the church must see themselves as having the righteousness of God in Christ, in accordance with the word of God. The realization that the church is constantly being purified by the Blood of Jesus from worldly, anti-spiritual pollutants and recognition of its holiness in Him, is essential to the inner purification of the church of believers. The people of God must also edify each other through exhortation, fellowship and mutual encouragement.

Ephesians 5:27 ______________________________

1 Thessalonians 5:11 ______________________________

Hebrews 3:13 ______________________________

Colossians 3:16 ______________________________

3. The Outward Relationship

The church is called to live out God's purposes not in isolation but rather in the world and in society. Failing to acknowledge and execute a relationship with society will jeopardize the original plan of God for the church. As the transforming agent of the world, we are commissioned to carry the love of God to every one in every nation. Some churches choose to withdraw themselves from the affairs of the society and to remain aloof from the world. But, the church is an advocate on behalf of God to speak Biblically to societal issues.

Matthew 28:19-20 ______________________________

Matthew 5:13-16 ______________________________

Questions for Discussion

1. What are the fundamental causes for the existence of your church?
2. How does your church accomplish the mission of God?
3. Mention few tangible approaches undertaken by your church to live out God's purposes?
4. What are the factors that hinders the growth of the church?
5. What steps can be taken to become a healthy church so as to fulfil the divine call?

Chapter 7

The Kingdom of God and Christian Missions

The significance of the entity called the kingdom of God is inseparable from Christian mission. Understanding the kingdom of God leads to a more complete knowledge of the mission of God. The central theme of Jesus's ministry, particularly to the Jews, revolved around the kingdom of God. His teachings on the Kingdom of God included the message of repentance, the assurance of God's love, goodness and blessings toward kingdom citizens, kingdom obligations, and the hope of their eternal future. There is no possibility to comprehend any missional efforts without rooting ourselves with the principles of the kingdom of God. This chapter will provide us the basic summary of the kingdom of God and its possible implications for Christian missions today.

Definition of the Kingdom of God

Ladd's thesis defines the kingdom of God as, "the redemptive reign of God dynamically active to establish his rule among men, and that this kingdom, which will appear as an apocalyptic act at the end of the age, has already come into human history in the person and mission of Jesus to overcome evil, to deliver mankind from its power and to bring them into the blessings of God's reign."[32] Alfred Edersheim wrote that the Kingdom of Heaven/God "is the whole Old Testament sublimated, and the whole New Testament realized."[33]

The Kingdom of God in the Old Testament

The concept of the kingdom of God in the Old Testament indicates God's plan of building and establishing an eternal kingdom. God was preparing the nation of Israel which had no identity, status or significant background, to show forth His divine purposes.

1. Covenant Centered Kingdom

Unlike the structure of a manmade kingdom, the kingdom of God was rooted and established by His own initiative to make a loving covenant with people.

Exodus 20:2-3 ____________________________________

Exodus 19:3-6 ____________________________________

2. The Eternal Kingdom

The Kingdom of God in the Old Testament always pointed to the future eternal kingdom. God was preparing His people so that they could live as a holy people by the standards of His eternal future kingdom and to ultimately receive Jesus in the fullness of time.

Psalms 145:11-13 ________________________________

Daniel 4:3 ______________________________________

Micah 4:7-8 _____________________________________

Daniel 2:31-45 ___________________________________

---

[32] E. Roger Hedlund, *God and the Nations* (Delhi: ISPCK, 2008), 202.

[33] John Bright, *The Kingdom of God: The Biblical Concept and its Meaning for the Church* (Nashville: Abingdon, 1953), 197.

3. The Davidic Kingdom

God's purposes for His kingdom were reflected in the purposes of the kingdom of King David. Burrows says, "In the promises of God to establish David's kingdom forever we see the extension of the earthly into the eternal. God promised to David far more than a line of human successors on his throne: 'And thine house and thy kingdom shall be made sure for ever before thee: thy throne shall be established forever.'"[34]

The Kingdom of God in the New Testament

The teaching of the kingdom of God is explicitly delivered in the New Testament and it can be described by the following titles:

1. Actualization of the Spiritual Kingdom of God

Jesus pointed out not only the eschatological kingdom of God but also confirmed the kingdom of God among them. He taught that we have an eternal kingdom to look forward to, but at the same time, the realm of His kingdom can be truly actualized on this earth. The reality of the kingdom of God on earth assures us of the hope of the kingdom of God in eternity.

Matthew 12:28 ________________________________

Luke 17:20-21 ________________________________

Matthew 6:33 ________________________________

Romans 14:17 ________________________________

John 18:36-37 ________________________________

2. How to Qualify to Become a Kingdom Citizen

True repentance (turning to Jesus) and commitment to a new life of bearing fruit unto God by the outworking of His Power and by the indwelling of the Holy Spirit, are the key to entering the kingdom of God. Both John the Baptist and Jesus announced the nearness of

---

[34] Reg Burrows, "The Kingdom of God and Mission," *Churchman* 101.1 (1987) p. 7-8.

the Kingdom and invited the people to repent (i.e., turning to Jesus, from the old Law into His Grace) showing - to the great surprise of their hearers - that entry was not by Jewish parentage but by a spiritual change of heart.[35]

Matthew 3:2 ____________________

Matthew 4:7 ____________________

Matthew 13:11 ____________________

Matthew 17:11 ____________________

Acts 26:18-20 ____________________

3. Life in the Kingdom of God

The New Testament gives a significant amount of importance to life in the kingdom of God. The Sermon on the Mount characterizes the kind of people who live in the kingdom of God as those who bear the fruit of His divine life and righteousness in them. By adhering to these kingdom values, we display the values and purposes of His kingdom. Burrows rightly asserts, "Jesus's teaching makes it clear that life in the kingdom of God is essentially spiritual; the attitudes taught and the righteousness required are beyond the de sire, let alone the achievement, of the natural man."[36]

Matthew 5:19-20 ____________________

Matthew 18:21-35 ____________________

Matthew 16:17-19 ____________________

4. Various Aspects of the Kingdom of God[37]

Any kingdom has its unique characteristics. During His short span of life and ministry on earth, Jesus described the characteristics of the kingdom of God. He presented the message of the kingdom of God

---

[35] Burrows, "The Kingdom of God and Mission," 8.

[36] Burrows, "The Kingdom of God and Mission," 10.

[37] Brown, Rick. The kingdom of God and the mission of God, Part 1, p. 8. (https://www.ijfm.org/PDFs_IJFM/28_1_PDFs/IJFM%2028%201_Brown.pdf).

in a context that the people of Israel, who were under the suppression of Roman empire, could understand. Jesus's message provided them with necessary hope and courage to anticipate God's kingdom. The differences between a normal kingdom and the kingdom of God include:

	A Normal Kingdom	**The Kingdom of God**
King	Ruled by a king or queen.	Christ-ruled, a title which means the king sent by God to meditate his saving rule to His people.
Accession	A king receives kingship from his father or by appointment from a higher king.	The Messiah is anointed to be king by His Father, the great King.
Length of reign	A king rules for a period of time, usually until he dies.	The Messiah King lives and rules forever.
Royal Authority	A king has nearly absolute authority over his subjects, except as he is subject to rules handed down from his father or a higher king.	The Christ has nearly absolute authority over earth and heaven. He fulfills the will of his Father.
Rule	A king rules over his subjects, governing them, granting them privileges, and regulating aliens within his realm.	The Messiah King rules over his subjects, governing them, granting them privileges, and restraining aliens.
Government	A king appoints those who will help govern, conferring on them varying degrees of responsibility and status.	The Messiah King appoints those who will reign with him.

Body Politic (citizens)	A kingdom includes a body of citizens. Their citizenship permits them to live in the realm under the protection of the king's rule. Aliens enjoy fewer benefits.	The kingdom of Christ includes a body of citizens called the saints, the church, etc., who enjoy the blessings of the Kingdom. Aliens enjoy fewer benefits and will eventually be excluded.
Citizenship	There are criteria for being a citizen, including allegiance to the king or government, and a procedure by which an alien may become a citizen.	The criterion for citizenship is faith in Christ as the eternal savior-king. The outward sign of becoming a citizen is baptism.
Laws	Laws and traditions govern the behavior of a kingdom's citizens. By obeying the laws they exercise good citizenship	The "Kingdom law" is to love one's neighbor (James 2:8). Its ethos is "righteousness, peace and joy in the Holy Spirit" (Romans 14:17).
Service and Obedience	Citizens relate to their king as his servants (whereas, in a democracy, the government serves the people).	Citizens of Christ's kingdom are called to trust and obey him and to serve the Kingdom and its citizens.
Benefits	The king and his government provide services, maintain public order, and enforce right behavior.	The King provides forgiveness, eternal life, and "righteousness and peace and joy in the Holy Spirit."
Realm	There is a territory over which a king exercises his authority— over both the citizens and aliens living in it.	Christ has been given all authority in heaven and on earth.

Residency	Citizens have a right to reside in the king's realm.	Citizens have a right to reside in Christ's kingdom in heaven.
Gatherings of citizens	Citizens are allowed to participate in local assemblies of citizens, which in Greek were called an ecclesia.	Citizens of the Kingdom of God on earth gather in local assemblies, which the Greek NT calls an ecclesia. This is translated into English as 'a church.'

The Kingdom of God and Christian Mission

The teachings of the kingdom of God are essential for the understanding of the Christian mission today. It provides us with objectives, obligations and assurance to take God's mission on this earth forward. Mission exists to assist in actualizing the eschatological kingdom of God and helps us eagerly anticipate the future eternal kingdom of God. Below are listed a few key aspects of Christian mission where kingdom values and teachings are the foundational elements.

1. Evangelism

It is a response to the call towards the accomplishment of the Great Commission of Jesus Christ.

Matthew 18:19-20 ________________________________

2. Word-Centered Mission

Mission demands complete trust in the sufficiency of the Word of God (Jesus is the Word made flesh). It is the essence of God's message for humankind without which we cannot understand the heart of God.

Isaiah 55:9-11________________________________

Matthew 13:1-9 ________________________________

1 Peter 1:22-25________________________________

Hebrews 5:12-14 ________________________________

3. The Kingdom Citizens as the Salt and Light

The church cannot carry out its God-given purposes and mission without its understanding and expounding the teachings of the kingdom of God. The Kingdom of God has been inaugurated in the Person of Jesus Christ. Padilla asserts, "Church cannot be properly understood apart from the presence of the kingdom. The mission of the Church is an extension of the mission of Jesus - it is the manifestation (though not yet complete) of the Kingdom of God, through proclamation as well as through social service and action. The apostolic witness continues to be the Spirit's witness to Jesus Christ as Lord through the Church. God, who placed the whole universe under Jesus, 'appointed him to be the head over everything for the Church, which is his body, the fullness of him who fills everything in every way.'"[38]

Ephesians 1:22-23 ______________________________

Ephesians 2:10 ______________________________

Matthew 5:13-15 ______________________________

Questions for Discussion

1. Why Jesus' teaching on the "Kingdom of God" is significant?
2. Elaborate on the relationship between the kingdom of God and the mission of God?
3. What are the obligations of a kingdom citizen to accomplish God's mission?
4. How can you transform your community with the help of Jesus' teaching on the kingdom of God?
5. What is the role of your church as the salt and light of the earth?

---

[38] C. Rene Padilla, "The Mission of the Church in Light of the Kingdom of God." Transformation Apr.-Jan. 1984, 10.

Chapter 8

Migration and Christian Missions

India as a nation is experiencing enormous change in all dimensions of society, especially in the last few decades which have seen significant socio-cultural and economic reforms. Advancements in technology, modernization and globalization are the principal factors driving significant transformation in India. People from all strata of society have directly or indirectly felt the impact of the modernization of India, as tremendous economic growth has facilitated migration of people from remote and rural areas to the emerging urban cities throughout India. At the same time, the rate of international migration has also grown exponentially.

This chapter briefly describes the concepts and factors that contribute to the migration occurring in India. In addition, a Biblical overview of migration is presented so that local churches can understand and prepare to effectively minister to migrant communities in India.

Definitions of Migration

Migration is "a form of geographical or spatial mobility between one geographic unit and another, generally involving a change from a place of origin or departure to a place of destination or arrival."[39]

Human migration is one of the most complex components of population change. It provides an important network for the diffusion of ideas and information, indicates symptoms of social and economic change, and can be regarded as human adjustment to economic, environmental and social problems.[40]

Population migration is described as an expression of interaction over space but differs in certain essential characteristics from other channel of interactions, mainly in terms of the commodity which is being transported.

Population migration is described as an expression of interaction over space but differs in certain essential characteristics from other channel of interactions, mainly in terms of the commodity which is being transported.[41]

Migration is an indicator of racial, linguistic and nationalistic mixing of the earth's population.[42] Migration is an instrument of social diffusion and cultural integration so that it may create communities within the community.[43]

Migration is the part of the wider study of population geography and is an important element in the understanding of the geographical organization of human society.[44]

---

[39] M. Hassan, Population Geography, (Jaipur: Rawat Publication 2005), 281.

[40] Demko, G.J-Ross H.M and Schnell, G.A. "Population Geography: A Reader," (New York: McGraw Hill Book Company, 1970), 286-287.

[41] Kirk Dudley, major Migration since world war 2 in - Demko, G.J-Ross H.M and Schnell, G.A. "Population Geography: A Reader" (New York: McGraw Hill Book Company, 1970), 300.

[42] O.S Srivastava, "A text Book of Demography" (New Delhi: Vikas Publishing House Private Ltd, 1983), 157.

[43] Srivastava, "A text Book of Demography" 157.

[44] P.E Ogden, "Migration and Geographical Change" (London: Cambridge University Press,1984).

Types of Migration[45]

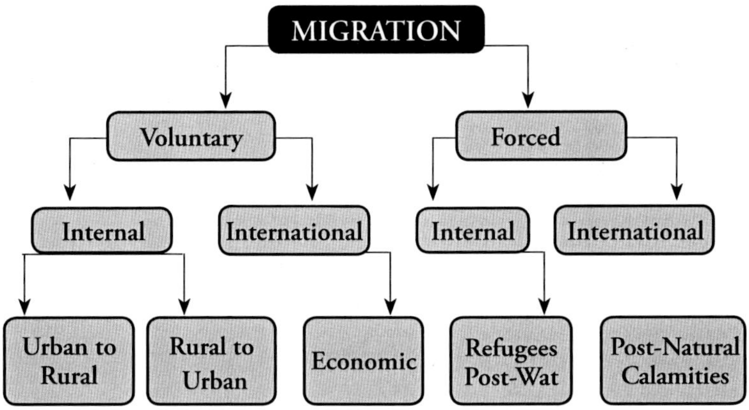

The above diagram illustrates the types of migration based on two factors, popularly known as "Pull Factor and Push Factor." These two factors help categorize migration and identify the ultimate causes behind it. The diagram above also draws our attention to two kinds of migration which are widely known as "internal migration" and "international migration."

Internal migration is defined as the change of residence within national boundaries such as between states, provinces, cities or municipalities. An internal migrant is someone who moves to a different administrative territory.[46]

International migration refers to the change of residence over national boundaries. An international migrant is someone who moves to a different country. International migrants are further classified as legal immigrants, illegal immigrants and refugees. Legal immigrants are those who moved with legal permission of the receiver nation, illegal immigrants are those who moved without legal permission and refugees are those crossed an international boundary to escape persecution.[47]

---

[45] Picture: http://gsekkes.com/Population%20Geography.htm.

[46] http://family.jrank.org/pages/1169/Migration-Types-Migration.html.

[47] http://family.jrank.org/pages/1169/Migration-Types-Migration.html.

Internal Migration Rate in India

The census 2011 indicates the rate of positive and negative net migration happening in various states of India. The net migration rate can assist in tracking the number of people coming to their administrative territory and the people of moving towards new administrative territory within India.

According to the census of 2011, the rate of migration to the major states of India has increased more rapidly than ever before, and is due largely to urbanization of a few states. As the result of the rapid pace of urbanization, rural India is gradually changing into urban India. Even the rural towns and villages are expanding and are becoming larger towns and cities where the impact of urbanization is felt in all spheres of society.

One significant research study conducted by the Indian government reports that, "out of about 98 million total intra-state and inter-state migrants in the country during the last decade, 61 million have moved to rural areas and 36 million to urban areas. The migration stream out of rural areas (73 million) to other rural areas was quite high (53 million) compared to migration from rural to urban areas (20 million). About 6 million migrants went to rural areas from urban areas. Based upon the number of migrants by last residence during the past decade, (i.e., the difference between in – migration and out – migration) in each state, Maharashtra stands at the top of the list with 2.3 million net migrants, followed by Delhi (1.7 million), Gujrat (0.68 million) and Haryana (0.67 million) as per census. Uttar Pradesh (-2.6 million) and Bihar (-1.7 million) were the two states with the largest number of net migrants migrating out of the state."[48]

Factors for Internal Migration in India

There are various causes of the accelerated rate of internal migration in India. Internal migration refers basically to the change or transition of residence within the national boundaries, from one administrative location to another. Most of the causes of internal migration are due to two types of migration driven by "Push Factors and Pull Factors."

---

[48] http://censusindia.gov.in/Census_And_You/migrations.aspx.

Push factors compel people of one administrative location to move to another location due to persistent problems or unexpected occurrences. Some examples of push factors are unemployment, poverty and natural calamities. On the contrary, pull factors are causes that attract people to migrate towards cities and urban areas where they can find solutions to their existing problems and a better life. High salary, suitable employment, and provision for advanced lifestyles are examples of pull factors. Listed below are some key causes of internal migration found in India that are influenced by push and pull theory of migration.

1. Urbanization

Urbanization is the fastest phenomenon occurring in India today. Urban populations now comprise a huge percentage of people from rural India. Industrial development has introduced new platforms for the expansion of various industries primarily in the cities. Along with industrialization, the rate of employment has correspondingly increased. This is the major driving force behind the enormous increase in migration to cities. Unemployed people from rural India are availing themselves of opportunities to make their dreams to true. Aghamkar presents the report of the Ministry of Urban Development, "India is in the midst of a gigantic urban increase, claiming to have fifty-three cities with a million plus population."[49] Migration to cities assures the migrants of a sense of economic security.

2. The Institution of Marriage

The sacred institution of marriage is one of the social factors which has resulted in increased migration. Regardless of geographical distance, most newly-wedded brides must migrate to their in-law's house. Sometimes, in the case of inter-caste or interstate marriage, we see not only the geographical movement of an individual from one area to another, but also witness the cultural convergence of the individual within that new state.

---

[49] Atul Y Aghamkar, "Migration, Change And Christian Mission Among Migrants", p. 2. https://www.academia.edu/6055520/MIGRATION_CHANGE_AND_CHRISTIAN_MISSION_AMONG_MIGRA NTS.

3. Aspiring for Quality Education

Some of the more brilliant minds of India hail from the remotest parts of rural India. In the majority of instances, the brightest individuals fail to realize their potential for success due to their lack of a quality education. The privatization of education has had a great effect on India's educational system. However, quality education has concurrently become so expensive that potential candidates cannot afford to study. In the 2011 census, about 1.77 percent of people in India migrated to obtain a better education, says Dr Anju.[50] Due to poorer educational facilities and lack of advancement at rural government educational institutions, many good students are compelled to migrate to urban areas in pursuit of their dream educations.

Impact of Internal Migration in India

Migration provides new opportunities in many areas, but at the same time, it can expose people to potential problems, especially for the migrants in unfamiliar territory and circumstances. At the same time, the migrant's original territory can face economic and social upheaval because of the departure of the native people. Listed below are some of the major, immediate as well as long term effects of migration.

1. Unhealthy Living Conditions

A large section of migrants from rural villages to urban cities are from the labor class. Their main reason for migration is to obtain higher wages. Their desperation compels them to settle down in undesirable areas of the cities. Ravi Srivastav rightly asserts that, "in spite of the Contract Labor Act which stipulates that the contractor or employer should provide suitable accommodation to the laborers, they still continue to live in sub-human conditions. Apart from the seasonal workers, workers who migrate to the cities for jobs live in parks, on the pavements, and become slum dwellers, and most migrants stay in deplorable conditions, with inadequate supplies of water

---

[50] Anju Bala, Migration in India: Causes and consequences (International journal of Advanced Educational Research, Volume 2, Issue 4, p. 55.

and bad drainage facilities."[51] The poor quality of daily life amidst these unsatisfactory living conditions paves the way for an increase in severe clinical disease and threats to their security and very lives because of crime infestation in their neighborhoods.

2. Familial Relationships

The family is the primary unit of society and it is an important channel of change and growth. Indian communities are known worldwide for their joint family structure where a huge number of immediate and extended family members live under one roof. Due to rapid growth in urbanization and its diverse impact, this prevailing family structure is now taking another course. Atul Aghamkar asserts that "the tempo of industrialization considerably influences the structure and functions of family. It transforms the family into a unit of consumption, the function of production being taken over by industries and occupations associated with them. One of the most visible impacts of urbanization is the trend from the traditional to the nuclear family. Though the traditional joint or extended family still persists in urban India, the trend toward the nuclear family is gaining strength."[52] There has been a significant amount of concern about the heavy increase of nuclear families since this challenges the familial bonds of the traditional joint family structure.

3. Environmental Change

Internal migration in India has largely impacted the environment of its cities. Large scale migration impacts the existing urban population and especially its residential settlements. Dr Anju Bala says, "It causes haphazard growth of cities and causes slums lacking basic infrastructural facilities such as safe drinking water, electricity, sewage etc. Overcrowding is also responsible for many environmental problems of air, water, land and noise pollution, and

---

[51] Ravi Srivastava, "Impact of Internal Migration in India" (Migration out of Poverty Research Consortium, Center for the study of regional development, Jawaharlal Nehru University, New Delhi) p. 10.

[52] Y. Atul Aghamkar, Migration, change and Christian mission among the migrants, p. 12-13. https://www.academia.edu/6055520/MIGRATION_CHANGE_AND_CHRISTIAN_MISSION_AMONG_MIGRA NTS.

for the management and disposal of solid waste."[53] It becomes a challenge for the government to keep changing the existing policies due to the large number of migrants and new migrant communities. As the government is well aware of urbanization and its scope for growth in cities, it needs to prepare for the changes which can occur because of migration.

4. Socio-cultural Shifts

Indian urban cities have become multi-cultural and social centers for diverse communities from all around India. Directly or indirectly, they share their worldviews and social norms and beliefs which have their own unique consequences. Migrants accumulate more knowledge and experience in the shared platform of urban cities. Dr Anuj Bala rightly says, "It breaks the narrow thoughts and widens the mental horizon of the people. Throughout history, India has received migrants from different cultural groups causing cultural changes, but sometimes migration creates a social vacuum and sense of dejection among individuals who then fall in crime and drug abuse."[54]

5. Economical Change

A huge section of people from the Indian rural population migrate to urban cities in order to earn higher wages in compared to their local areas. This group of migrants either go for a short term occupation or settle down in the cities for a long period of time. Due to the larger scope of employment opportunities, migrants pave their own ways to get into any company or their desired work. Many governmental policies and laws are also affecting people and their livelihoods and survival. Atul mentions Kopardekar's listing of various government acts and laws that have affected the rural and small-town people including the Tenancy Act, the ceiling on ownership of farming land, Minimum Wages Act, the prevention of bonded labor, liquidation of rural indebtedness laws, and laws protecting depressed classes from

---

[53] Anuj Bala, "Migration in India: Causes and consequences", Vol. 2, Issue 4, 2017. International Journal of advanced educational Research. p .56.

[54] ibid., 55.

unscrupulous large landholders and money lenders.[55] When these laws are enforced in rural areas, the people are often compelled to migrate to urban cities.

Bible and Migration

Paying specific attention towards migrants was one of the key commands given by God in the Scripture. Migration is an ancient reality and has continued throughout human history. Several occurrences regarding the safety and care of migrants in the Bible convey God's heart, His plan and His purposes for them. The Biblical references and insights listed below show God's concern for the migrants and inspire us to consider the migrant communities as one of our key mission goals as well as a channel of carrying God's mission.

A. "Ger", the Hebrew word closest to "immigrant/migrant" in English, appears 92 times in the Old Testament. The people of God are called to seek after love and justice for the immigrants.

Deuteronomy 10:17-19 ______________________________

B. Many biblical characters were immigrants and were used mightily by God. The world relief made a presentation.[56]

a. Abraham: Called by God/Fled famine
b. Rebekah: Family Based immigrant
c. Joseph: Victim of human trafficking
d. Ruth: Fled famine
e. David: Asylum seeker
f. Jesus: Refugee
g. Paul: Employment based immigrant

---

[55] H. D. Kopardekar, Social Aspect of Urban Development. A case Study of the Patterns of Urban Development in the Developing Countries (Bombay: Popular Prakashan, 1986), 147.

[56] Notes simplified from Justice, Compassion, & Truth in the Immigration Debate Presented by John Faison.

C. God's laws to ensure safety, dignity and equality for the immigrants.

Deuteronomy 24:14 ____________________

Exodus 20:10 ____________________

Deuteronomy 24:15 ____________________

Leviticus 20:2 ____________________

Leviticus 24:16 ____________________

Exodus 23:9 ____________________

D. God is mindful towards the oppression and injustice of the helpless and foreigners/immigrants and will come to aid in the time of their need.

Psalms 146:9 ____________________

Zechariah 7:10 ____________________

Jeremiah 7:6 ____________________

E. God reminds His people of their own status as the foreigner

Exodus 23:9 ____________________

Leviticus 19:33-34 ____________________

Deuteronomy 10:19 ____________________

F. The Great commission of Jesus Christ inspires us to reach every nation with the good news.

Matthew 28:19-20 ____________________

G. The movement of people is not an accident but part of God's plan to draw people to Himself. (Urbana).

Acts 17:26-27 ____________________

The Church's Concern Towards Migrant Communities

Since the migrant population is currently greatly increasing, the church has a good opportunity to reach people from various backgrounds with the love of Jesus Christ. As a transforming agent for the kingdom of God, it must reassert its vision and calling in the world. It must come out of traditional legalistic coldness and respond to the needs of believers through the grace of God. If the church does not respond to societal change in a way that shows Jesus's heart and grace, it will not win those who are in desperate need of salvation. In his classic work, Stanislaus, SVD, categorizes the church's responses to migrants in India in the following key areas:

1. Strengthening Pastoral Care

Migrant communities are often neglected in the area of proper pastoral care, in spite of the local church's great concern for migrants. Pastoral care of migrants requires not only enthusiasm, but also self-development of the pastors because they must understand the needs of the target migrant group. Stanislaus believes that "the socio-cultural context of migrants requires a radical pastoral conversion from the auto-referential and repetitive paradigm of looking after souls, to a more creative missionary approach in evangelism. Moreover, when migrants are particularly numerous and present as a homogeneous group, they should be encouraged to keep their culturally-specific traditions. Any organized religious assistance must be tailored to the language, culture and rites of the migrants."[57] General pastoral care of migrants will not impact them for Jesus as much as contextual evangelism will impact them. Pastors must frequently reevaluate their strategies for reaching migrants in order to keep their efforts properly focused on culturally-specific needs and context.

2. Expressing Solidarity

Solidarity with migrants requires our willingness and commitment to incarnate ourselves in their own context. Church being a separate entity of born-again believers who are sometimes isolated from

---

[57] L. Stanislaus and Jose Joseph. "Migration and mission in India". (Delhi: Ishvani Kendra/ISPCK), 233.

migrant life realities will sometimes not achieve an effective level of ministry among them unless pastoral care is conducted with the feeling of oneness with the community. Believers in the faith community must be able to translate their lives and thinking into the context of the incoming migrants. Campese asserts that, "it is to allow the migrants and refugees to challenge our cultural and religious prejudices and our often untested convictions... It means to be opened to changes, open to complexity of life, to the surprise of life, and to a God full of surprises."[58] Such vital commitment to migrants requires reconsideration of our inherent convictions and the nature of the divine calling, so that we in local churches can apply God-given wisdom in evangelizing migrants, all for the glory of God.

3. Careful Inculturation/Interculturation

The developing urban church must pay special attention to inculturation. Migrants come into an existing church community with their own prejudices, cultural worldview and social beliefs. However, one of the most important and obvious principles that must be adhered is that the Gospel is always above any cultural and social framework. It has the ability to address and cater to the need of any diverse context. The church cannot compromise the faith with alien beliefs and worldviews of pagan migrants. Monteiro says, "dialogue between cultures as a tool for overcoming ethnocentrism and promoting esteem for one's own identity as well as that of others- is synonymous with respect for diversity, acceptance of difference, and with appreciation of riches found in other's history, cultures and spirituality."[59] The pursuit of ministry among the migrants must include enabling migrants to appreciate their God-given identity and dignity, but must disparage divisive issues that are not Biblically supported.

58 Cioacchino Campese, 'walking Humbly with Your God! Notes on spirituality for Missionaries with Migrants" Sedos, vol. 29, no. 11(1997), 290-296.

59 Evelyn Monteiro, "Church and Culture: Communion in Pluralism" (Delhi: ISPCK, 2004).

Questions for Discussion

1. Migration is an opportunity or challenge? Discuss both views?
2. What are the possible causes of migration in your state?
3. Elaborate your church's response to people's migration in your communities?
4. Why do you think that your church must address the issue of migration and how the local church has been impacted by this?
5. Mention your church's action plans for the smoother transition and pastoral care of the migrant communities?

Chapter 9

Developing Cross-Cultural Communication

The rise of technological advancements and their ability to physically and socially connect people in different geographical locations within a few hours or minutes, has accelerated the process of globalization. The entire world has now become a global village. Despite this incredible advancement, communication among people groups is still difficult because of their cultural differences and diversity of backgrounds. There is a growing need for the development of cross- cultural communication in most sectors of Indian society. In Christian ministry, cross-cultural communication is key to successful church planting, growth and mission enterprise. This requires development, and understanding, of cultural worldviews that govern behavior patterns. The study of cross-cultural communication helps ensure healthy and fruitful communication by endowing us with cultural competence.

Definition of Cross-Cultural Communication

The phrase "cross-cultural communication" describes the ability to successfully form, foster and improve relationships with members of a culture different from one's own.[60] Cross-cultural communication thus refers to the communication between people who have differences in any one of the following: styles of working, age, nationality, ethnicity, race, gender, sexual orientation, etc. Cross cultural communication can also refer to the attempts that are made to exchange, negotiate and mediate cultural differences by means of language, gestures and body language. It is how people belonging to different cultures communicate with each other.[61]

The Bible and Communication

Communication is the essence of human relationship. An ability to communicate is the direct outcome of a healthy physiological development. The process of communication is the essence of socialization and networking. Without any doubt, the Bible can be considered as the communication handbook of God to humankind. That communication is one of the key spiritual essentials, is supported by Scripture. Some examples are presented below:

Sutherland opines that, "we communicate because God communicates. Francis Schaeffer has shown that within the Trinity, there was both communication and love. Jesus had glory, and the love of the Father before the creation of the world. The Father communicated to the Son that Jesus was to go into our world. There was knowledge of each Person of the Trinity. The Word had fellowship with God before coming to earth. The Spirit is also eternal, and was present with the Father and Son from the creation of the world."[62]

Genesis 1:26 ______________________________

John 1:3 ______________________________

John 17:5,24 ______________________________

Col 1:16 ______________________________

---

[60] Josephine_https://wecommunication.blogspot.com/2014/09/cross-cultural-communication.html.

[61] https://www.communicationtheory.org/cross-cultural-communication/).

[62] Famadv/crosscul.doc/ 1/2/1998 Jim Sutherland.

Imago Dei is a term that reflects the human ability to communicate. Since man was created in the very image of God, he possesses God-given attributes, including the ability to communicate. A person's ability to communicate with others is based on the reality of God creating him in His own image.

1. The Bible is Multi-Cultural

The entire Bible is a story of God engaging with people from all cultures. The message of His love remains constant for all, regardless of their differences. God's Word has the capability to speak to all generations by catering to their contextual needs. Since all are created in the very image of God, Ted Ward, a missiologist, claims that our similarities and commonalities always outweigh our differences. He further says, "The image of God rests on all people. All people have a longing for eternity in some form, for instance. God has given people consciences, which reflect another attribute shared with God, morality. Humans also love, which reflects God. People also have an aesthetic sense--we appreciate sunsets and art. We enjoy beauty because God made that beauty. He himself is beautiful. He is extravagant with that beauty, creating flowers that none will ever see but Himself."[63]

Genesis 1:27 ____

Ecclesiastes 3:11 ____________________________________

Romans 2:14-15 _____________________________________

I John 4:8 ____

2. The Bible is Supra-Cultural

In today's world, there have been many attempts to judge Biblical values from a cultural perspective. But the Bible is above any culture, which implies that it has the power to address any emerging cultural issue. Jesus declared that the cultural assertions of Samaritans regarding the place to worship to be absolutely wrong. Paul wrote, "Even one of their own prophets has said, 'Cretans are always liars,

[63] https://www.rmni.org/files/global/Cross_Cultural.PDF.

evil brutes, lazy gluttons.' This testimony is true. Therefore, rebuke them sharply, so that they will be sound in the faith." However, in the same chapter, Paul gave behavioral guidelines for the selection of elders, which were in complete harmony with those given to Timothy for other cultures, illustrating absolute moral criteria."[64]

John 4:19-22 ____________________

Titus 1:12-13 ____________________

Titus 1:5-9 ____________________

1 Timothy 3:1-7 ____________________

Ralph Winter's Model of Cross-Cultural Communication[65]

The well-known scholar Ralph Winter has proposed three models of cross-cultural communication for evangelism, which he calls the E-1, E-2 and E-3 models of communication.

1. E-1 Model of Communication

This model of communication is limited to one cultural group of people. Winter says, "it is essentially a communication of the Gospel to members of one's own cultural group, that is, people speaking one's own language and whose cultural values are known to one." This model of communication is very common and found everywhere. For example, the local church takes the initiative to reach the people of the native culture.

2. E-2 Model of Communication

Ralph Winter describes, "it is the communication of the Gospel to people who either speak your own language but belong to another subculture than you, or whose language and culture is known to you and resembles your culture so that you can communicate without great effort." For instance, we find the existence of several subcultures

---

[64] Famadv/crosscul.doc/ 1/2/1998 Jim Sutherland.

[65] J A Van Rooy, Cross-Cultural Communication 0f The Gospel, 2-3. https://www.koosvanrooy.co.za/theological-articles.html).

in a specific region in India. Even though their language is different, there is similarity with the primary culture of that land.

3. E-3 Model of Communication

This model of communication seems to be very difficult as it relates to a different culture. Ralph Winter rightly asserts that, "it is a communication of the Gospel to people of whom both the language and culture are unfamiliar to the communicator." Winter pointed out in his address, mentioned earlier, that this type of evangelization is still the most neglected type. In addition, he pointed out the shocking fact that by far most missionaries are engaged in preaching the Gospel to people belonging to the E-1 group, and furthermore, not to self-confessed unbelievers, but to nominal Christians within the E-1 group. Since this model of communication model requires the greatest effort from the local missionaries, it is the least explored and the most neglected model of communication. For this reason, there is an urgent need of development in, and for the application of, the E-3 model of cross-cultural communication so that the skills of our native missionaries and church planters will be improved enough to penetrate the different cultural territories.

Barriers of Cross Cultural Communication

Cross-cultural communication involves active engagement with other cultures. There are many barriers to this process. Careful attention to these barriers helps create a path for successful cross-cultural communication. Some of the key barriers are listed below.

1. Ethnocentrisms

It is one of the biggest barriers to cross-cultural communication, developed over a period of time, acting as a wall of separation between individuals. In general terms, it categorizes a culture as being between "us" and "them". A person who belongs to the same culture is classified as being in the "in" group, while a person in another culture is classified as being in the "out" group. It always gives the priority to the "in" group. There is a misunderstanding that "out of group" culture is junior or inferior to the culture of the "in" group.

Ethnocentrism judges the another person's culture based upon the standards and values of the "in" group. Those who believe and who are influenced by ethnocentrism usually exhibit poor cross-cultural communication skills. Moreover, they create barriers for themselves and cause schisms in their relationships.[66]

2. Language

Language is the essential medium of communication. People using the same language convey their emotions, ideas and opinions in a uniform, commonly understood manner; and most importantly, they identify themselves with a specific culture and region. "Sometimes it seems common when misunderstanding is created among people who speak the same language. Therefore, it is not astounding that people who belong to other regions, cultures and linguistic backgrounds can have misunderstandings. Moreover, mispronunciation of a word with a lack of specificity can become a communication barrier. When people speak a language intangibly in any organization, it takes listeners a huge amount of time to comprehend the intended meaning of the speaker."[67]

3. Values and Beliefs

Every individual grows with his own values and beliefs. The influence of family, the growth environment and education, etc., all shape one's values. Everyone possesses a set of values and beliefs. In the modern era, various regions, cultures and languages have tremendous impacts on the shaping of values. Effective cross-cultural communication requires an in-depth understanding of people from, and with, different cultures, regions and languages.

4. Stereotypes

A stereotype is a very harmful obstacle to cross–cultural communication. It is an assumption that one person makes about other persons based on their culture, race, gender, nationality, and/

---

[66] https://www.ukessays.com/essays/business/barriers-cross-communication-3173.php.

[67] A paraphrase of https://customwritings.co/barriers-of-cross-communication/.

or ethnicity. Basically, stereotypes arise due to lack of knowledge and fear about the other person. Stereotypes occur when a person does not communicate well due to his feeling of self- consciousness or shyness because of his perceived minority status and culture.

Consequences of Cross-cultural Barriers in Christian Ministries

1. Ethnocentrism in Christian ministry tends to promote ones' ethnicity over that of others. Gradually, the dominant ethnic values and beliefs are imposed upon the minority. As a result of such forceful imposition, division and conflict can arise among them all.
2. Diversity of language can be a great blessing if it is used as a collective ministerial achievement. Since India is a land of diversity, there are many different languages within one region. These sub-languages are slightly different in their pronunciation and slang. A loose and careless pronunciation of a word can mean something disrespectful to others. A successful cross-cultural minister/worker will try to acquaint himself with these language issues in order to ensure effective communication without causing problems.
3. Values and beliefs can very subjective in nature and can vary from one region to another or from one culture to another. In the mission field, cross-cultural missionaries and Christian workers will come across very different values and belief systems. If they are not flexible enough to learn about the values and beliefs of others, they may end up judging the behavior of others. It is one's set of acquired and nurtured values that governs their human behavior. A cross-cultural communicator will always recognize this reality and respect and safeguard the values of another, as Biblically appropriate, in daily interactions.
4. Cultivating the habit of using stereotypes is unacceptable in Christian ministries. It violates the basic Christian principle of honoring the image of God in the individual. A person who encourages stereotyping people defines and judges them based on their upbringing or value-based behavior. Fostering such

negative attitudes toward others can assassinate their personhood and make it more difficult for them to see themselves as sons and daughters of God and heirs with Christ.

Resolving Cross-Cultural Communication Barriers

1. A good cross-cultural communicator in any form of Christian ministry has the ability to listen empathetically. Patient listening results in greater understanding.
2. Being surrounded by several cultures in India, we have a vast platform for cultural learning. Our cultural competencies will greatly minimize the barriers among cultures and will enable us to become good communicators.
3. A fact-oriented and detail-oriented individual will generally gain expertise in cross-cultural communication very quickly. This expertise greatly lessens the chances of misunderstanding.
4. An effective cross-cultural communicator will exhibit a great amount of enthusiasm for new knowledge. He always challenges his traditional frame of mind and updates himself with knowledge and information on the emerging cultures.
5. Sam Behar says, "we can be honest about our own cultural bias and open a dialogue about the differences that exist between our culture and the culture of the people we are serving. While it seems like a small thing, this may be the best way to find out what you are doing 'wrong.'" (Overcoming the Barriers to Healthy Missions: The Culture Barrier). The knowledge of culture in all its diversity is a tremendous help to reach the unreached people of the world. Cross-cultural communication is one of the key catalysts of world evangelism. Even though there have been several initiatives from various Christian institution and organizations to promote cross-cultural communication, they are insufficient to meet the need. Christian mission requires more and better training in cultural competence and more effective tools for healthy, Biblical cross-cultural communication.

Questions for Discussion

1. Explain on the importance of cross-cultural communication for Christian ministries?
2. If you are a cross-cultural missionary/or worker, then mention few practical and actionable steps which can ensure effective communication?
3. Does your church include people from diverse background? If yes, what are the challenges for the effective communication?
4. Explain the importance of training in cultural competence for the Christian workers in ministries?
5. In the light of your own context, prepare a model of effective communication?

Chapter 10

Contextualization and Christian Missions

Contextualization is an integral part of Christian mission. It helps to translate the Gospel message in an understandable format within a specific cultural context.

Definitions of Contextualization

Contextualization is an effort to express the never changing Word of God in ever-changing modes for relevance to contemporary situations. Bruce Fleming states that, "Since the Gospel message is inspired but the mode of its expression is not, contextualization of the modes of expression is not only right but necessary."[68]

According to Von Allmen, contextualization is new terminology developed to "express the fact that the situation of theology in a process of self-adaptation to a new or changing context is the same in Europe as in Asia or in Africa." Therefore, he adds, "The problem of the birth of theology in a new context remains unchanged."

---

[68] Bruce C.E. Fleming, Contextualization of Theology: An Evangelical Assessment (Pasadena: William Carey Library, 1980), 62.

Bruce J. Nicolls defines contextualization as ". . . the translation of the unchanging content of the Gospel of the kingdom into verbal form meaningful to the peoples in their separate culture and within their particular existential situations."[69] Taber uses indigenization, accommodation, and contextualization as synonyms and defines these terms as "a process, sometimes intentional and sometimes unintentional, by which a message which is initially alien takes on a shape more congenial to the total receptor context."[70]

The Significance of Contextualization

Since contextualization plays a pivotal role in communicating the Gospel meaningfully and in a relevant manner, there is a clear affiliation between mission and contextualization. Jackson Wu proposes four profound reasons for our unavoidable need of contextualization of the Gospel message in Christian mission.

1. Contextualization Spreads and Preserves the Gospel

Jackson Says "Contextualization shapes every aspect of the Christian life. It is more than a missionary strategy, a narrow evangelistic concern. Contextualization refers to the process wherein people *interpret*, *communicate*, and *apply* the Bible within a particular cultural context." Being communicators of the Truth, when we properly contextualize the Gospel in a culturally relevant manner, we can promote Jesus and His work and the essence of the Gospel to everyone.

2. Life in its Entirety

According to Jackson, "we contextualize the Gospel in order to make disciples, not converts. Therefore, Biblical contextualization seeks to transform people's entire view of the world, not merely their religious affiliation and traditions." The ultimate goal of contextualization

---

[69] David J. Hesselgrave and Edward Rommen, "Contextualization: Meanings, Methods and Models" (USA: William Carey Library, 2013), 33.

[70] Charles R. Taber, "The Limits of Indigenization in Theology," in Readings in Dynamic Indigeneity, ed. Charles H. Kraft and Tom N. Wisley (Pasadena: William Carey Library, 1979), 372-399.

must be the total transformation of an individual, rather his mere superficial engagement with the Good News. Jesus came to give us Life, and Life more abundantly.

3. All Nations

The God of the Bible has been often accused of being a Western God. Jackson suggests that one reason for this accusation is that people (e.g., missionaries) typically share the Gospel in a rather Westernized manner. This does not imply that "Western theology" is somehow bad or false. However, a traditional Western contextualization of the Gospel is merely one way of presenting it. This is understandable since even the Biblical authors vary in how they express the gospel.

There must be an intentional and collective initiative to meaningfully present the Word to all nations through appropriate Biblical contextualization of God's message to individual culture.

4. Encompasses all Generations

The relevancy of God's message for all generation is unchangeable. In the process of cultural and Biblical contextualization, we sometimes observe certain gaps between the communicated message and its recipient. Contextualization that has both Biblical integrity and cultural relevance will promote long-term results and maturity in the new believer instead of merely short-term results.

Useful Factors in the Application of Contextual Theology

Contextual theology and related teaching should take several crucial factors into account in order to enhance their effectiveness. Ross Langmead cites several of these important factors which are listed below.

1. The Gospel Itself

Langmead says, "Biblical revelation comes fully clothed in culture. There is no such thing as a non-cultural Gospel. The Gospel comes only in culturally-expressed forms. We can't strip it back and see it in its purity, because it only comes in incarnational form, enfleshed in particular places, times and people."[71] The Gospel has the power to incarnate in any culture and context. It can never be disqualified simply because it was first given in a Greco-Roman background.

2. The Culture of Biblical Revelation

Our understanding of, and contextualization of, the Bible requires a good understanding of the culture of the Bible in its original languages. Langmead believes that, "Biblical studies are an essential tool in contextual theology. Recent biblical theology has been exciting in directing attention not only to literary forms, but also socio-cultural factors in the writing." (Langmead, 53).

3. Relationship with Jesus and the Gospel and the Holy Spirit

Many times we might claim to have received the purest and fullest form of the Gospel and there are no other ways to look at it. However, "to communicate sensitively in a cross-cultural context, we need to become aware of our own limitations, and be humble about the partial understanding we have. The more we learn about other ways of seeing the Gospel, the more we can assess our own limiting cultural and sub-cultural factors,"[72] writes Langmead. The more we understand the relevance of the Gospel from diverse perspectives, the better we are able to communicate its power to save, heal, and deliver individuals in cultures different than our own.

4. Native Cultures

The culture that we live in greatly influences our understanding of the Gospel. The worldviews and values in which we grow up can act as spectacles with which we view and color our understanding of the Gospel message. However, when we exhibit the willingness to embrace new, Spirit-driven perspectives, we can truly impact non-native cultures.

---

[71] Langmead, Ross. Journal of Tribal Studies, Vol II, No. 1, January to June 1998, 53.

[72] Ross. Journal of Tribal Studies, 54.

5. Receptor's Cultures

Contextualization pays close attention to the culture of the recipients. Langmead expresses that, "The 'receptor culture' will have elements that distort the Gospel and elements which express the Gospel more adequately than the culture of those sharing the Gospel. We are not very good at respecting, learning about and re-casting the Gospel into other cultures. This is true even of sub-cultures within our own culture." With contextualization, the essence of the Gospel must be safeguarded by the consideration and incorporation of only valid and true principles from the recipient's culture.

Three Approaches to Contextualization

Paul Hiebert presents three essential approaches to contextualization. Every form of contextualization falls in anyone of these three categories. Regardless of cultural differences, these three approaches can be used in the process of the contextualization of the Gospel.

1. Non-Contextualization

Langmead discusses Hiebert's approach and states that: "This is the view that the gospel is above culture and needs little adaptation between cultures. Few Christians take this point of view now. Even the most conservative missiologists, who would want to say that revelation is largely supra- cultural, that is, above culture, agree that it must find its expression within various cultures. Hiebert also pointed out the possible consequences of non-contextualization and said that Christianity is seen as a foreign religion and is therefore rejected. Secondly, local customs, condemned by missionaries, go underground, and we have a problem with a hidden parallel religious expression, which is syncretistic."[73]

With the non-contextualization approach to presenting the Gospel, more attention is given to Biblical revelation than for the need for its expressions in various cultural forms. This approach simply suggests the individual should embrace Biblical revelation

---

[73] Ross Langmead, "Mission and contextualization" *Journal of Tribal Studies*, Vol II, No. 1, January to June 1998, p. 56-57.

and truth as it is written, without any attempt to contextualize the Biblical revelation and truth.

2. Uncritical Contextualization

The second approach of contextualization allows the local traditional practices inside the church. It shows great respect for one's own culture and rejects any domination of Biblical revelation and teaching in other cultures. Langmead analyzes this "Hiebert" view and points out several of its shortcomings. First, uncritical contextualization fails to recognize that the Gospel addresses the fact that there are corporate and cultural sins as well as personal ones; and that while Jesus' Blood cleanses us from all of these sins, oppressive practices such as slavery, widow-burning, foot- binding, caste, human sacrifice are clearly areas where the Gospel calls for cultural transformation. All men are valuable because God so loved them that He sent His Son, and thus every individual is to feel secure, significant and special to God. Secondly, this second approach of uncritical contextualization can lead to syncretism since people may continue in old practices and beliefs and these can eventually become mixed into their new Christian beliefs, perhaps in a form of Christo paganism."[74]

The level of the challenges which emerge due to syncretism is governed by the lack of uncritical contextualization. It is important that we Scripturally evaluate any and all cultural elements infiltrating the life of the local church so that there will be little chance of syncretism and so that Biblical authenticity is preserved.

3. Critical Contextualization

Critical contextualization addresses the need of individuals within the church to biblically evaluate all aspects of daily life and invites them to properly and Scripturally internalize old cultural ways. We must help new believers learn Bible truths and gather information without critical or judgmental attitudes towards them. This is known as the phenomenological method, which suspends beliefs until information is gathered and processed. "This is best done with the people, listening to their myths, watching their rituals etc...

---

[74] Ross. Journal of Tribal Studies, 57.

Study the Bible in relation to the issue at hand, aware that we as leaders are also culturally-biased. Allow the congregation to critically evaluate their own past customs or beliefs in the light of their biblical understandings, and decide themselves what they think and will do. They will sometimes reject old practices, sometimes modify them and sometimes keep them. The theological foundations for this trust are three fold: The priesthood of all believers, the authority and effectiveness of the Bible, and the work of the Spirit through the church."[75]

Questions for Discussion

1. How do you define contextualization?
2. Why do we need to Contextualize in Christian ministries?
3. Explain your method of contextualization in the ministries?
4. What are the barriers of contextualization, narrate from your experience?
5. Suggest few actionable strategies for relevant and meaningful contextualization?

[75] Paul G. Hiebert, "Anthropological insights for missionaries" (Grand Rapids: Baker Academic, 1985), 191-192.

Bibliography

Andrews, Edward D. "Reasoning from the Scriptures: Sharing Christ as you help others to learn about the mighty works of God." USA: Christian Publishing House, 2018.

Bala, Anju. Migration in India: Causes and consequences (International journal of Advanced Educational Research, Vol. 2, Issue 4, 55.

Bosch, David. "Transforming Mission: Paradigm Shifts in Theology of Mission." New York: Orbis Books, 2006.

Bright, John. *The Kingdom of God: The Biblical Concept and its Meaning for the Church*. Nashville: Abingdon, 1953.

Burrows, Reg. "The Kingdom of God and Mission." *Churchman* 101.1 (1987), 7-8.

C.E. Bruce Fleming. Contextualization of Theology: An Evangelical Assessment. Pasadena: William Carey Library, 1980.

Campese, Cioacchino. 'walking Humbly with Your God! Notes on spirituality for Missionaries with Migrants" Sedos, vol. 29, no.11(1997), 290-296.

Demko, G. J-Ross H.M and G.A. Schnell. "Population Geography: A Reader." New York: McGraw Hill Book Company, 1970.

Dudley Kirk, Major Migration since world war 2 in - Demko, G.J-Ross H.M and Schnell, G.A. "Population Geography: A Reader." New York: McGraw Hill Book Company, 1970.

George W, Peters. *A Biblical Theology of Missions.* Chicago: Moody Press, 1988. George W, Peters. *A Biblical Theology of Missions.* Chicago: Moody Press, 1988. Hassan, M. Population Geography. Jaipur: Rawat Publication, 2005.

Hedlund, E. Roger. *God and the Nations.* Delhi: ISPCK, 2008.

Hesselgrave David J. and Edward Rommen. "Contextualization: Meanings, Methods and Models." USA: William Carey Library, 2013.

Hiebert, Paul G. "Anthropological insights for missionaries." Grand Rapids: Baker Academic, 1985.

Kane J. Herbert. Christian Missions in Biblical Perspective. Grand Rapids: Baker House, 1976.

Keller, Tim. "Contextual and Missional," Lecture Three of the Urban Plant Life series of the London Church Planting Consultation, 2008-2009.

Kopardekar, H. D. Social Aspect of Urban Development. A case Study of the Patterns of Urban Development in the Developing Countries. Bombay: Popular Prakashan, 1986.

Lum, Ada. *A Hitchhiker's Guide to Missions.* Downers Grove: Intervarsity Press, 1984. Manokaran, J N. "Christ and Transformational Missions." Chennai: Mission Educational Books, 2008.

McGavran, Donald A. *Understanding Church Growth.* Michigan: Wm. B. Eerdmans Publishing Company, 1980.

Monteiro, Evelyn "Church and Culture: Communion in Pluralism." Delhi: ISPCK, 2004. Moreau, A. Scott, Gary R. Corwin and Gary B. McGee. *Introducing World Missions: A Biblical,*

Historical, and Practical Survey. Grand Rapids: Baker publishing group, 2004.

Neill, Stephen. "How my mind has changed about mission", Video recording produced by Oversees Ministries Study Center, 1984.

Ogden, P. E. "Migration and Geographical Change." London: Cambridge University Press,1984. Padilla, C. Rene "The Mission of the Church in Light of the Kingdom of God." Transformation Apr.-Jan. 1984, 10.

Peters, George. *A Biblical Theology of Missions*. Chicago: Moody Press,1984.

Radmacher, Earl D. *What the Church is all About: A Biblical and Historical Study*. Chicago Moody Press, 1978.

Ross. Langmead. Journal of Tribal Studies, Vol II, No. 1, January to June 1998, 53. Srivastava, O. S. "A text Book of Demography." New Delhi: Vikas Publishing House Private Ltd, 1983.

Srivastava, Ravi. "Impact of Internal Migration In India." Migration out of Poverty Research Consortium, Center for the study of regional development. New Delhi: Jawaharlal Nehru University.

Stanislaus L. and Jose Joseph. "Migration and mission in India." Delhi: Ishvani Kendra/ISPCK.

Taber, Charles R. "The Limits of Indigenization in Theology," in Readings in Dynamic Indigeneity, ed. Charles H. Kraft and Tom N. Wisley. Pasadena: William Carey Library, 1979.

Tenny, Merrill C. *Zondervan Pictorial Encyclopedia*. Grand Rapids: Zondervan, 1976.

Wilkins, Michael. "Following the Master: A Biblical Theology of Discipleship." Zondervan Publishing House: Grand Rapids, Michigan.

christianitytoday.com/edstetzer/2014/october/what-is-contextualization American Heritage Dictionary.

gotquestions.org/syncretism-religious. https://www.krusekronicle.com/kruse_kronicle/archives.html#.XQh76IgzbDdNature and Mission of the church: A Stage on the way to a common statement, WCC publication, Faith and order paper 198, Geneva, p. 8. (https://ecumenism.net/archive/wcc/2005_wcc_fo_nature_mission_church_en.pdf).

Image taken from https://upper-register.typepad.com/blog/2012/09/how-do-church-and-mission-relate.html, dated 7th Feb., 2019.

Brown, Rick. The kingdom of God and the mission of God, Part 1, p. 8 (https://www.ijfm.org/PDFs_IJFM/28_1_PDFs/IJFM%2028%201_Brown.pdf.

http://family.jrank.org/pages/1169/Migration-Types-Migration.html.

http://family.jrank.org/pages/1169/Migration-Types-Migration.html.

http://censusindia.gov.in/Census_And_You/migrations.aspx.

Aghamkar, Atul Y. "Migration, Change And Christian Mission Among Migrants", page 2 https://www.academia.edu/6055520/MIGRATION_CHANGE_AND_CHRISTIAN_MIS SION_AMONG_MIGRANTS.

Josephine_https://wecommunication.blogspot.com/2014/09/cross-cultural-communication.html.

Picture: http://gsekkes.com/Population%20Geography.htm.

https://www.communicationtheory.org/cross-cultural-communication/).

Famadv/crosscul.doc/ 1/2/1998 Jim Sutherland.

https://www.rmni.org/files/global/Cross_Cultural.PDF.

Famadv/crosscul.doc/ 1/2/1998 Jim Sutherland.

J A Van Rooy, Cross-Cultural Communication of The Gospel, 2-3.

https://www.koosvanrooy.co.za/theological-articles.html).

https://www.ukessays.com/essays/business/barriers-cross-communication-3173.php.

A paraphrase of https://customwritings.co/barriers-of-cross-communication/.